# O. & W.

## The Long Life and Slow Death of the New York, Ontario & Western Railway

*40th Anniversary Edition*

by
**William F. Helmer**

D1560279

BLACK·DOME
**1011 Route 296**
**Hensonville, New York 12439**
**Tel: (518) 734-6357**
**Fax: (518) 734-5802**
**blackdomepress.com**

Published by

Black Dome Press Corp.
1011 Route 296
Hensonville, New York 12439
Tel: (518) 734-6357
Fax: (518) 734-5802
blackdomepress.com

ISBN 1-883789-25-7


Library of Congress Cataloging-in-Publication Data:


Helmer, William F.
    O & W : the long life and slow death of the New York, Ontario & Western Railway / by
William F. Helmer.-40th anniversary ed.
        p. cm.
    Includes bibliographic references.
    ISBN 1-883789-25-7 (trade paper)
    1. New York, Ontario, and Western Railway Co.-History. I. Title.

    HE2791.N653 H4 2000
    385'.06'5747-dc21                                                                00-034279

Cover design by Carol Clement, Artemisia, Inc.
Printed in the USA

Cover illustration: Midnight at Middletown, by Otto Kuhler

10 9 8 7 6 5 4 3

# DEDICATION

For Joan and the boys (Bill and Steve)
And the later additions (Mary Claire and Michael),
Altogether a family to be proud of

## PREFACE
## TO THE 40TH ANNIVERSARY EDITION

THE TEMPTATION to tinker, to remedy imperfections or to seek other improvements in a new edition can be great, but for the most part I have resisted that impulse. The original work, written with a sense of loss and disbelief, I have left to stand as the quirky historical chronicle it was. And the sentiments to be found in the previous prefaces reflect that rather personal viewpoint. I, and many others, miss that old railroad. Younger generations too may find reasons here to miss, as we do, the grand pageant that they can only envision.

The first edition of this book had the benefit of a dedicated (and patient) professional team, Morgan and Flora North of Howell-North Books. Their talents, especially the editorial skills and mastery of layout and design of Flora, made that first edition a most attractive work. After the death of Morgan North, their much-praised firm sold out to another reputable publishing house which, in turn, sold out to another. Then, during a corporate crisis in which an entire editorial staff was terminated, a second edition came off the press, with little or no editorial oversight. Consequently, the final product was a disappointment.

Then, after thirty years in print, *O&W* disappeared—along with its last publisher. Only through the persistent detective work of Deborah Allen of Black Dome Press did the page negatives come to light. She and assistant Steve Hoare have now restored the original luster of that first printing with their considerable skills and artistic sensibilities.

One change, which not all will notice, is the addition of two names to the dedication, to account for most welcome additions to our family after the book's 1959 publication.

To all who pick up this book, I invite you to read, relive, remember or recreate and thus enjoy some of what was best of the past.

William F. Helmer
Morrisville, New York
April, 2000

# CONTENTS

# ILLUSTRATIONS

# ACKNOWLEDGMENTS

THE COOPERATION of the following individuals has made this book possible:

Reed Alvord

Hope Emily Allen

Ira Avery

Mrs. R. O. Barber

Miss Dorothy C. Barck,
Librarian, New York State
Historical Association

Edward Baumgardner

Jay C. Baxter

Lucius Beebe

Gerald M. Best

Mrs. Albert Billings

Frederick Bonke

Thomas E. Brochu

William Brock

Glenn Buell

Stanley J. Bulsiewicz

Fred Cagwin

William Capach

Oliver Carruth

Harold H. Carstens

Jesse D. Caryl

Miss Ida M. Cohen,
Assistant Librarian, New York
State Library

Milton E. Conkling

C. B. Conrow

Stanley D. Crews

Pierre DeNio

Charles Diebold

DeForest Diver

Mrs. Bessie Everhart

John Fagan

Howard L. Fairchild

Jack Farrell

Charles E. Fisher

Mrs. Edith Fox,
Curator and Archivist,
Cornell University Library

Mrs. Lewis D. Freeman

Herbert J. Gabriel

Thomas B. Girard

Harold Goldsmith

William R. Gordon

Dr. Charles F. Gosnell,
State Librarian, New York
State Library

Mrs. Robert Griffiths,
Librarian, Morrisville Library

Samuel E. Grover

Robert F. Harding

Ivon Harris

Henry Harter

Mr. James Heslin,
Assistant Director, New York
Historical Society

Homer House
H. I. Humphrey
Robert Humphries
Wilson Jones
Pearson M. Judd
Mrs. William C. Kessler
Lee G. Kibbe
Sterling O. Kimball
Karl Korbel
Eugene F. Kramer,
  Curator of History, New York
  State Education Department
Otto Kuhler
Bob Larson
John Lawson
Eric Light
Walter A. Lucas
Frederic E. Lyford
Eugene Magner,
  Librarian, Institute at
  Morrisville
Stephen D. Maguire
William F. Mathieson
Roger Mattes
Mrs. Mildred McKay
David P. Morgan
Elwin Mumford
Thomas Natoli
Professor Allan Nevins
E. H. P. Gilman,
  Assistant to the President,
  New York, Susquehanna &
  Western Railroad
Joseph H. Nuelle

Elbert N. Oakes
Walter Osgood
George Phelps
Albert Phillips
H. Louis Purdy
R. T. Reidenbach
Joseph E. Rinaldo
Captain Winfield Robinson
Harry Sanford
Karl E. Schlachter
William H. Schmidt, Jr.
Jim Shaughnessy
Dr. Thomas Sinclair,
  Association of American
  Railroads
George C. Slawson
Joseph A. Smith
Professor Charles M. Snyder
Edward Stanley
John Stellwagen
Mosie C. Stratton
Herbert Mussman
F. W. Tanneberger
Paul W. Tilley
Albert E. Tompkins
Earl Towne
Harold K. Vollrath
John C. Walsh
Otto Weiss
Harold M. Whiting
William S. Young
George Younglove
Guy K. Weeden

# PREFACE

THE WRITING of this book has been both a sad and pleasant task; sad because it records the end of an era, pleasant because it has acquainted me with the loyalty and affection of a host of O&W friends and employees. Although the troublesome and cantankerous little railroad has passed from the scene, its days of glory live on in the minds and hearts of thousands. A large segment of this faithful group supplied me with the raw materials and the encouragement out of which this history has come.

The story told here makes no attempt at completeness — such an attempt would take a lifetime of labor and result in a multi-volume work. Neither does this book presume to be a corporation history — such an approach would miss the pulsing life of the gallant line and reduce the story to a mass of meaningless statistics. What is presented here is a selection of the events, the individuals and the anecdotes which gave the Ontario and Western its special appeal, its individuality, its uniqueness among the family of American railroads. If I have re-created the atmosphere that distinguished the Old and Weary, then my goal has been achieved.

The satisfactory completion of this history depended to a great extent upon the cooperation of the individuals listed in the Acknowledgments. To these persons and to hundreds unnamed I owe a debt of thanks. In addition to these, I must acknowledge the assistance of the Research Foundation of State University of New York for a grant enabling me to obtain secretarial assistance and to defray travel expenses. The secretarial assistance was most ably supplied by Mrs. Charles Townsend; the transportation was furnished rather grudgingly by a vintage Dodge. I wish to express my further appreciation to Mr. Royson Whipple, Director of the Institute, for assigning me extra office space and for extending numerous other courtesies. Two of my colleagues have been most generous with their help: Professor Frank Leaden drew the maps and Mr. Arthur Hicks provided valuable photographic aid. Last of all, I am grateful for the infinite patience of my wife.

*State University of New York*          WILLIAM F. HELMER
*Institute at Morrisville*
*August 1, 1959*

CHAPTER ONE

A RAGING EPIDEMIC spread across the United States after the Civil War, carrying its infectious influence far from the centers of population, straight into the tiny hamlets and the homes of isolated farmers. The disease itself lasted a short time—a few years at the most—but its consequences may be felt down to the present day. The malady, of course, was railroad fever. Dreams of enormous profits, of great commercial activity, of tremendous national expansion captured the minds of farmers, merchants, bankers, day-laborers, and manufacturers. The latent possibilities in the extension of these iron networks taxed a man's imagination.

Here was the answer to muddy, rutted rural highways, to the incredible slowness of the canals, to the monotony of rustic living, to the sameness of one locality. The 19th century observer, gazing down a slender, curving embankment, or appraising a lofty timber trestle, found a beauty here like that of the rainbow or the evening sunset. The promise of the railroad was an infinite one.

Almost every "progressive" community clung to a pet project that would connect it with the outside world. Nowhere was this desire for an outlet more pronounced than in that large area lying between the lines of the New York Central and the Erie. Among the mountainous regions of the Catskills, in the rolling hills along the Chenango and on the flat lands around Oneida Lake enthusiastic citizens clamored for a direct rail link with the great metropolis to the south. A modern reader of the yellowed newspapers of the period receives the distinct impression that railroad surveyors were so thick in upstate New York that they stood shoulder to shoulder and tripped over each other's feet. Possible routes through Sullivan County had been explored by Colonel Edward W. Serrell and a party of engineers as early as 1853. Disorganized agitation for a railroad continued for several years until 1865, when a correspondence sprung up between leading lights of Norwich, Delhi and Monticello, each encouraging the other in preliminary plans for a railway through these villages.

These civic boosters thus set the stage for an exciting railroad panorama—the saga of the O&W. The scene came alive with colorful characters and miscellaneous machinery, commencing almost a century of alternating hope and heartache, prosperity and poverty, dignity and degradation. The New York, Ontario & Western, the name which headed the obituary, was a railroad of contrasts. It claimed the most enthusiastic of friends and earned the bitterest of enemies. For thousands who followed her fortunes, the appeal of the gallant little line rests upon the battle fought against overwhelming odds as much as upon classic locomotives and magnificent scenery.

When the last sad train rumbled south to the graveyard at Middletown and after the faded depots had been padlocked for the final time, an era came to an end. The roots of O&W failure may be found in an American society obsessed with the iron horse and the iron trail.

On Wednesday, October 4, 1865, eager and hopeful delegates from the counties of Oswego, Onondaga, Madison, Cortlandt, Chenango, Delaware, Sullivan, Orange, Otsego, and Ulster, as well as representatives from New York City, met at Delhi, New York. The need for better transportation was emphasized by the October 3rd blizzard, which blocked the Brock Mountain Highway, the main route to Delhi. The survey through Sullivan County aroused heated debate from the Rondout (Kingston) group. With more foresight than they knew, these partisans deplored the planned line as impractical for several reasons. They cited the steep grades and long tunnels, the poor and sparse population, and finally, the lack of all kinds of financial support. With considerable parliamentary finesse, adherents of the Sullivan route maneuvered a recess for dinner at 4 p.m. Many of the Rondout faction were local farmers who found it necessary to forego the evening session because of chores. In their absence, the issue was no longer in doubt — the "impractical railroad" would be built. Samuel Gordon of Delaware County was privileged to present the formal resolution:

> Resolved: That a railway through the counties of Onondaga, Chenango, Otsego, Delaware, Ulster or Sullivan, and Orange, on or near the surveys made some twelve years ago, to some point on the Hudson River, is a state and local necessity for the transportation of merchandise, manufacturing, agricultural and mineral productions—and must be made.

In December, answering those critics who favored the Hudson River line, Gordon stated:

> The right men had got hold of it now—men who would not sell out to the Central or any other road. An airline can be built without reference to immediate location, no dodging to hit this or that locality, and no right angles to strike the Hudson, or please anybody, or aid any interest. What was wanted was an independent, and the straight line between the two cardinal points named. [Oswego and New York]

How well these admirable principles were carried out may be judged by subsequent developments, and especially, by a quick glance at the meandering right-of-way on the map. Within a few years after this statement was issued, the memory of it would bring grim smiles to the faces of discouraged men.

The next meeting of the railroad committee was held at the Saint Nicholas Hotel in New York City, having been transferred from the almost inaccessible Delhi. Two days of spirited discussion brought two hitherto silent partners into the scheme —Henry R. Low and Dewitt C. Littlejohn.

Of the two, the self-made Littlejohn proved to be the more dynamic personality. A former mayor of Oswego and a merchant of substance there, he had tilted with the renowned Horace Greeley of the *New York Tribune*. As an early supporter of the stillborn Syracuse and Susquehanna Railroad and other similar projects in the State Legislature, Littlejohn was subjected to vitriolic criticism not only from Greeley, but from the famous abolitionist-statesman, Gerritt Smith. His position as Chairman of the Committee on Commerce and Navigation, plus his post as Speaker of the Assembly, gave him unprecedented influence in railroad matters. Tall, slim and intense, the man was a commanding platform speaker, radiating sincerity and self-confidence. Few could miss the resemblance to the late martyred Lincoln. Wherever he spoke to railroad meetings, his audience fell under the spell of his piercing eye and his accusing finger. How could these hypnotized natives resist the "golden opportunity" so glowingly offered?

The partnership was a good one, for Henry Low was an able attorney, a member of the State Senate, and although a less persuasive orator, he was considered one of the best debaters in Albany. As Littlejohn represented the northern terminus, he stood for the southern, Middletown.

Maps and profiles of the New York and Oswego Midland, as it had been named, were exhibited by Colonel Serrell and sufficed to dispel most remaining doubts. Littlejohn was appointed to draw up articles of association and the committee adopted a resolution requesting state aid in the form of a town bonding law.

When next the organization met in Albany, Edward Palen of Sullivan County reported on the collection of funds necessary for formal incorporation under New York State law. The required 10% had been obtained, and the corporation was officially formed. Inevitably, D. C. Littlejohn was elected president, and the project to construct a steam railroad from Oswego to New

Promoter and supersalesman, Dewitt C. Littlejohn built a railroad "at right angles to the mountains."

# ARTICLES OF ASSOCIATION

## OF THE

# New York and Oswego Midland Railroad Company.

The subscribers, being desirous to form a Company, under and in pursuance of the Law of the State of New York, authorizing the formation of Companies for the purpose of constructing, maintaining and operating railroads for public use in the conveyance of persons and property, and entitled, "An Act to authorize the formation of Railroad Companies and to regulate the same," passed April 2d, A. D. 1850, and of the several acts amendatory of the same, do make and sign these ARTICLES OF ASSOCIATION in compliance with the requisitions of the aforesaid act and the amendments thereof.

FIRST.—The corporate name of the Company shall be the

"NEW YORK AND OSWEGO MIDLAND RAILROAD COMPANY."

SECOND.—The said Company shall continue for one hundred years.

THIRD.—The said Company is to construct, maintain and operate a Railroad from the City of Oswego, in the County of Oswego, and State of New York, to the State line of the State of New Jersey, and thence to a point on the Hudson River, opposite to the City of New York.

FOURTH.—The length of road to be constructed by this Company is not to exceed Two Hundred and Twenty-Five miles, and it is intended that the said road shall run through the Counties of Oswego, Onondaga, Madison, Cortland, Chenango, Otsego, Delaware, Ulster, Sullivan and Orange, in the State of New York.

FIFTH.—The amount of the Capital Stock of said Company shall be TEN MILLIONS OF DOLLARS, and shall consist of One Hundred Thousand Shares of the par value of One Hundred Dollars per Share.

SIXTH.—The names of the Thirteen Directors of the said Company, who shall manage its affairs for the first year and until others shall be elected in their places, together with their respective places of residence, are as follows:

"DeWitt C. Littlejohn, residing at Oswego; John Crouse and Gershom P. Kenyon, residing at Syracuse; Elisha C. Litchfield, residing at Cazenovia; Joseph W. Merchant, residing at DeRuyter; Edward T. Hayes and John A. Randall, residing at Norwich; Apollos C. Edgerton and Samuel Gordon, residing at Delhi; Henry R. Low, residing at Monticello; Edward Palen, residing at Fallsburgh; Homer Ramsdell, residing at Newburgh; and Nathan Randall, residing at Homer.

Each of the subscribers hereto agree to take the number of Shares of Stock in said Company, set opposite their respective names.

IN WITNESS WHEREOF, the subscribers hereto have hereunto set their hands this 13th, day of December, 1865.

| Names. | Residence. | No. of Shares. | Amount. |
|---|---|---|---|
| H. & J. Conn?? | Norwich | 4 | 4 00,00 |
| Chas. Hopkins. | Norwich | 3 | 300,00 |
| Samuel C Teal | Norwich | 3 | 300.00 |
| J. H. Eastman | Norwich | 3 | 300 00 |
| P. H. Butter | Norwich | 3 | 300 00 |
| Saml Rogers | Norwich | 3 | 300, 00 |
| H Goodrich | | 3 | 300.00 |
| Robert Harkness | | 3 | 300.00 |
| James Shetteplace | | 3 | 300 |
| D L Follett | | 3 | 300. |
| J. Bailey | | 3 | 300 |

York and from Norwich to Buffalo was under way. Headquarters were established at Oneida, New York. Thus began the tremendous undertaking that was to be known to people along the line as the "Midland."

Low, Littlejohn's second-in-command, stood in the Legislature on April 5, 1866 to introduce the so-called "Town-Bonding Act," providing for the issuance of town bonds not in excess of 30% of the assessed value of property within the town, in order to invest the proceeds in Midland stock. The bill also provided for a ten-year property tax exemption for the new road. Such was the enthusiasm of the law-makers (who reflected the feelings of a large segment of New York State voters) that the bill was passed on the spot. The monumental task of raising forty million dollars for the railroad's construction now began.

When articles of incorporation were filed on January 11, 1866, the physical description of the Midland showed that it would proceed from Oswego to the New Jersey state line, thence to a point on the Hudson opposite New York City. The engineering difficulties were enormous from the very first. The projected line of rail encountered steep grades between Norwich and Middletown, and whether to burrow through the mountains or cross them by means of switchbacks became a topic for serious debate. Nor were these construction problems the only ones which vexed the builders of the New York and Oswego Midland. The city of Syracuse, originally chosen as one of the stations on the route, refused to bond itself for $750,000, and the promoters, emulating the cantankerous James J. Hill and other railroad giants, shunned the Salt City completely by changing the main line to follow the northern shore of Oneida Lake. Unfortunately for the Midland, Syracuse had already established itself as a growing industrial center, and the sparsely settled lake country, in the words of an old-time railroader, "couldn't raise an umbrella." The expert in historical hindsight would have no trouble in spotting this move as one of the early tragic mistakes of the Midland management.

The year 1868 saw the first complete survey of the line. Busy agents of the company ranged through the countryside buying the right-of-way between the two terminals. Another stubborn community, Hamilton, declined to bond itself for the construction of the road. Here again the promoters showed their contempt for such an unwise move and realized the needed funds by shifting the main line so that it followed a rather steep grade over the hill to Eaton. Below the New York state border, all was in doubt, for New Jersey would not permit such bonding. The solution seemed to be the Middletown, Unionville and Water Gap, in operation for about two years, and a new railroad, originally touted as a coal carrier from Pennsylvania, the New Jersey Midland. The Oswego company simply did not have the resources to build this southern end. This fact could have been disputed by those who later discovered that Treasurer Walter Conkey earned as high as $100,000 a year in fees for negotiating the sale of town bonds, and who read in 1873 that Littlejohn was voted a salary of almost $150,000 for his seven years' service. In this early period, "economy" was not in the Midland vocabulary.

Railroad headquarters in Oneida became a beehive of activity. At the directors' meeting of February 6, 1868, William B. Gilbert of Albany was chosen chief engineer, and several committees from southern counties appeared to plead for branch lines. Littlejohn stipulated that such extensions would be built if $15,000 per mile were put up by these committees. No other consideration was of any importance, apparently. On March 26th, a general election was held which renamed Littlejohn president, Elisha P. Wheeler vice-president, B. Berry secretary, W. M. Conkey treasurer, H. R. Low attorney and W. B. Gilbert chief engineer. On June 2nd, steps were taken to transform the railroad on paper into a railroad in fact. Contracts were let for the Oswego to Oneida section to McNary, Clafflin & Co., Cleveland, Ohio; for the Oneida to Norwich section to Cephas Barker of Oneida and Jarvis Lord of Rochester; for the Norwich to

Sidney Plains section to Sage & Williams, Fulton; and all bridges to R. Cummins of Troy.

Within three weeks of the award of these contracts ground was broken at several locations along the line. On the Norwich and Sidney divisions an impressive band of personages met on the J. R. Wheeler farm southeast of the Chenango River at Norwich. After the Reverend Samuel Scoville had asked God's blessing on the venture, a workman, scrubbed and polished especially for the occasion, urged his team forward and the plow bit into the first earth moved on the grand new trunk line. Then an almost endless procession of bewhiskered officials and well-wishers moved a shovelful of earth. Short speeches by local notables were followed by a banquet at the Eagle Hotel. Similar ceremonies accompanied the beginning of construction at Durhamville, Oneida Community and Oneida, at about the same time.

The easiest part of the construction was now under way and only the southern portion remained. From a meeting in Middletown in September, contracts were given to Hitchcock & Co. of Oneida for the Bloomingburg tunnel, to Gage, Williams & Jerome for the New Berlin branch, and to Jackson & McDonald of Milwaukee for the Ellenville branch and the rest of the main line. Friends of the Midland looked at the survey maps and beheld a huge funnel through which upstate products would flow in abundance down to the great marketplace by the sea.

The most ambitious piece of work tackled by the new company was undoubtedly the Shawangunk tunnel at Bloomingburg. Begun in November of 1868, the bore (including entrances at each end) extended through five thousand feet of solid rock. A switchback over Northfield Mountain would solve the same problem at another natural barrier, and a slender iron bridge would vault the Lyon Brook gorge near Oxford. These were some of the major physical obstructions which the planners had to overcome.

The branch from Norwich to the west had not been forgotten. In December of the same year Midland surveyors were at DeRuyter locating the division known as the Western Extension. And the new year saw frenzied activity throughout the Midland country. Supplies began arriving at Sidney via the Albany and Susquehanna, at Oneida over the New York Central and at points along the Chenango Canal, which paralleled the railroad construction for a considerable distance. Conservative estimates place 2,000 men and 500 teams working directly upon the road between Oswego and Sidney Plains. Addison Day, an experienced railroader from the Rome, Watertown & Ogdensburg, became the new superintendent. The New Berlin branch started to take shape, as grading and the placing of ties and fence posts testified. Enthusiastic students from Madison University (Colgate) purchased $10,000 worth of Midland bonds, which demonstrated, in the words of a contemporary newspaper, "a commendable financial foresight upon their part, as well as a desire to help along a great work." The extensive bridge work necessary to cross Lyon Brook was taken over by Smith, Latrobe & Company, which contracted for wrought iron from the Phoenix Works of Philadelphia. Orders were placed early in the year with the Rhode Island Locomotive Works at Providence for the company's first motive power.

On April 24, 1869, the first locomotive to grace the new line arrived at Oneida. This high-wheeled beauty, with the ornate Rhode Island emblem displayed above her drivers, rolled from the New York Central yard astride temporary tracks laid down the center of Madison and Sconondoa Streets to the virgin rails of the Midland. Christened the *Oswego*, she had cost $15,000 and compared favorably with the best power on the Central road. It was not until the following June that *No. 5*, the *Sullivan*, arrived to share the work load with her sister engine. In the meantime, six miles of gleaming steel rails were spiked down to bear the weight of the shuttling *Oswego*. *No. 4*, the *Delaware*, took advantage of a transport facility she was

The slender iron span over Lyon Brook terrified Midland passengers. *No. 4*, the *Delaware,* has just run onto the bridge for one of the first trips across it.

*No. 1*, the *Oswego,* posed proudly in September of 1869 atop the Community (Kenwood) trestle over Oneida Creek.

soon to displace by floating on a canal boat to Constantia when construction was started north of Oneida Lake. Sherburne was the delivery point for *No. 2*, the *Madison,* and Sidney Plains for *No. 3*, the *Chenango.*

Farm boys along the fresh earth embankments found new heroes in the men who piloted these mammoth machines back and forth in the tedious chores of building a railroad. The names of these engineers have long been forgotten, but their weatherbeaten faces at the cab windows worked a magic that America has not known since the death of the steam locomotive. These Midland men deserve a place in this history. Thomas Wheaton was assigned to *No. 1*, Pat Crain to *No. 2*, Elam Cheesebrough to *No. 3*, Edwin Williams to *No. 4*, and Edward McNiff to *No. 5*—not saints, perhaps, but heroes nonetheless.

To keep these construction trains loaded with the impedimenta of building materials, the squat barges of the Chenango Canal disgorged large quantities of rails, bridge iron, timber and tools onto the landings. Accumulations of men added to the restless activity around the various construction depots. Laborers were drawn from the surrounding farms and villages and from the immigrants arriving at Castle Garden, the Ellis Island of the time. Low seniority employees on older railroads were tempted to try for OM positions as conductors or engineers. The Rome, Watertown & Ogdensburg supplied many of these skilled men, but they came from almost everywhere.

One of these trainmen was Heamon Purdy, a native of Utica, who returned homesick and disillusioned from his fireman's job on the woodburners of the old Hannibal and St. Joseph. After he was assigned to a work train, his 240-pound bulk became a prominent and solid fixture on construction and freight trains during the early years. Purdy soon acquired a reputation for his acrobatics atop the moving cars. Later in his Midland career, he is reported to have dropped a sheaf of waybills along the right-of-way near Munnsville as a result of walking the car tops on his hands. Burt Wells, his engineer, saw the papers flutter to the ground and reached for the engine brake. He was amazed to receive the portly conductor's signal to proceed, and even more startled to watch him reach down to pull the pin between the caboose and the last freight car. Setting the hand brakes hard, Purdy raced back to scoop up the papers, regained the caboose steps, released the brakes, applied a muscled shoulder to the little four-wheeled crew car and coasted downgrade to a perfect coupling with his train. Purdy was representative of the hard working railroaders who took their rough pleasure in horse-play and hearty humor.

The honor of running the first passenger train was given to engineer Edwin Williams and conductor James T. Purdy, when the *Delaware* drew a train of hop-pickers from Oneida to West Monroe. From this time onward organizations along the line began planning excursions and Sunday picnics over the rail-road. About the middle of September an inspection train hauled by engine *No. 8*, the *Oneida*, carried President Littlejohn and state and local dignitaries to West Monroe and returned. The single platform car was crowded on the return trip by groups of pipe-smoking Irish workers returning to their Oneida lodgings in the gathering dusk.

Amid the thunderous reports of cannon, the screaming of locomotive whistles and the cheers of hundreds of excited citizens, the last rail between Fulton and Norwich was laid on the evening of October 12th near Hamilton. With this much track-age in operation the projectors of the Midland could well congratulate themselves. But these railroad builders had visualized a grander scheme than the linking of upstate communities. Their avowed purpose was to construct an "air line" to the port of New York, and this portion below the Middletown, Union-ville & Water Gap was built by a separate corporation formed in New Jersey. When "consolidation" took place, President Cornelius Wortendyke of the New Jersey Midland was apparently slated for the number two post in the company administration.

*H. L. Purdy*

*H. L. Purdy*

H. H. Purdy and Thomas L. Foulkes were among the first conductors the Midland ever had.

The new railway swelled B. of L.E. ranks at Oswego. Leffin, Sanford and Harding were Midland men.

*Robert F. Harding*

## ～ 1874. ～
# Oswego City Division, 152,
# Brotherhood of Locomotive Engineers,
### Meets First and Third Sundays in each month,
### IN ENGINEERS' HALL,
## Midland Depot, Corner East Third and Bridge Streets.

### ～ OFFICERS. ～
### J. W. SUTTON, Chief Engineer.

F. WILLIAMS, *F. E.*   M. WELCH, *S. E.*,   C. B. SANFORD, *F. A. E.*

R. LEFFIN, *S. A E.*,   W. HUSTON, *T. A. E.*,   W. E. HARDING, *Guide.*

A. DONOHUE, *Chaplain.*   P. FENNELL, *Cor. Sec. and Jour. Ag't.*

## WELCOME TO THE WORTHY.

In these days of rapid progress, the laying of the last slim rail between construction points was the signal for local jubilation. Irish shovelers, seldom found under the temperance banner, were joined by jovial farmers, itinerant hop-pickers, town drunks, elated merchants and rustic mechanics in a round of toasts to the Midland. The politicians and company delegates to these festivities exhibited only slightly more restraint in their behavior; their imbibing was accompanied by somewhat politer deportment at a separate table in the nearest hostelry. No note of discord, except for the customary fist-fights, marred the proceedings, and most men conjured up their own brand of prosperity through an alcoholic haze.

When the junction was made between Oswego and Norwich, an inspection team made the first passenger trip on November 25th. Littlejohn, with Superintendent Addison Day at his side, rode in one of the newest coaches on the road. The gilded lettering, the red plush cushions, and the gleaming oak and walnut panels provoked hushed and reverent praise from the unofficial critics who gathered at rural stations all along the line. Before the party reached Oneida, however, a message was received that an embankment at Pratts had collapsed and was not yet repaired. Conductor Tom Foulkes took his train cautiously southward until they steamed up to the scene. From noon to 3 p.m., the passengers had a lesson in elementary digging and filling. When the embankment had been restored, a gravel train tested the new roadbed and escorted the official cars to Morrisville. On the way they met a strange procession consisting of an impatient brass band and chilled well-wishers who had felt that walking down the tracks would be more beneficial to circulation than waiting longer in the bitter winds outside Morrisville Station. These somewhat subdued marchers clambered aboard the cars and rode on to their station. A sumptuous repast was served to the official passengers at Norwich, where local legend has it that 100 rounds of cannon fire greeted the train's arrival. If the accounts of artillery salutes along the railroad are reasonably correct, upstate New York must have sounded like the Battle of Vicksburg for many months. When regular passenger service began, engineer Pat Crain and conductor James Purdy took charge of *No. 2,* which clattered and chuffed its way north with frequent pauses to "wood up." Other trains were run by Tom Foulkes, conductor and Ed McNiff, engineer; Tom Wheaton, engineer and P. Dietz, conductor; and E. Williams, engineer and R. Pendall, conductor.

The year 1869 came to a close with a magnificent occurrence. On December 29th a loaded passenger train from Norwich crossed the great Lyon Brook Bridge. With its long slender supports paired and crossed at the center, spaced at economic intervals, the trestle resembled nothing so much as a single file of drunken schoolmasters. Needless to say, it inspired little confidence. This engineering marvel was also called popularly the "Spider's Web," so that not all of the 700 passengers could be as daring as their presence would indicate. They could not be sure whether their audience of almost two thousand sight-seers from Norwich and Oxford were there to give them encouragement or to witness a catastrophe. Eyes wide and mouths agape, the spectators waited, their fears undoubtedly mixed with a lurking hope that they might be eye-witnesses to the greatest disaster in the history of American railroading. The engine *Fulton* with its drag of two passenger cars and ten platforms stopped at the northern end of the trestle to let the cowardly off. Then the train lurched forward and rumbled slowly onto the center span. At the exact center the locomotive clanked to a standstill and the whistle was sounded. How many feminine shrieks echoed that shrill call will never be known. The engineer crossed to the far side, then reversed and loaded those passengers who had declined the honor of crossing. These faint-hearted souls, who congratulated themselves upon having seen the crossing without hazarding their lives, were treated to a considerable surprise when they were jolted forward without warning, rocking across the bridge once more. This lightning passage was a safe one, however, and in a few moments they were backing slowly across Lyon Brook and returning, coaches and flatcars leading, through the outskirts of Norwich.

On one of the first Sunday excursions to Lyon Brook, Conductor Purdy added to his reputation as the "Midland Buffoon" by frightening his charges nearly out of their wits. Regularly a freight trainman, H. H. had taken the job of baggageman for the day. The practice was for the engineman to shut off steam and coast to an easy stop halfway across for a panoramic view of the gully. At the moment when the greatest number of noses were pressed hard against the car windows, an overall-clad figure hurtled out into space, made a graceful turn or two and smacked into the earth almost two hundred feet below. Gasps and screams expressed the horror of the passengers, and even when the blue denims were found to be filled with straw, many of the riders were not amused. Perhaps it was just as well that they didn't hear and see the guffaws and leg-slapping that went on in the baggage car. When the patrons' complaints had ceased and the officials' anger had cooled, Purdy was relieved to find that he still held his job.

The fears of the Midland's human cargo were not unfounded, for many a construction worker had given his life in the building of these timber bridges and perpendicular cuts. Working with icy hands in the sprawling wrought iron mass of Lyon Brook bridge was not an ideal way to spend the winter; the workmen who perished beneath tons of earth shaken loose from the almost vertical gashes in the hills contributed to the casualty figures for the early years of American railroading.

The completion of the Lyon Brook Bridge was only the first of several engineering accomplishments on the Midland. The great Shawangunk tunnel came back into the limelight when a nitroglycerin explosion killed a worker named Warren D. Hannum on May 5th. Excavation here proceeded at a steady pace, and a confident management resumed work on the De-Ruyter branch with an estimated 1,000 men and a steam shovel. President Littlejohn was quoted as saying that this offshoot would terminate on the shores of Lake Erie "without a doubt." On August 1st the little New Berlin branch was opened. By October the Utica, Clinton & Binghamton Railroad, which joined onto the Midland at Smith's Valley, was opened for its entire length. Before Christmas a lease of the UC&B was effected by the Midland and the Delaware & Hudson Canal Company. And this same month the sleepy hamlet of DeRuyter awoke one morning a railroad town, as the track layers pushed the rails as far as Tioughniogian Street.

The Midland brass hats were keeping pace with their construction crews by making agreements to furnish coal to upstate cities. These contracts led to the organization of separate companies like the Utica, Clinton & Binghamton and the Rome & Clinton. One more was planned—the Delhi & Middletown—but this line was never built, much to the chagrin of communities off the OM main line. Years later the village of Andes was striving in the courts to get the line constructed. The Midland's influence with the Chamber of Commerce of the State of New York led to appeals for state aid for the extensive tunnel work through the mountains. In the meantime, the firm of Simpson & Company of Mauch Chunk, Pennsylvania, was retained to build the remaining forty miles of OM trackage. These benevolent contractors let it be known that they had hired 100,000 Chinese to do the work. When this report had been duly publicized by gullible newspapers, the firm was able to hire native American workmen at extremely low wages. Nothing more was heard or seen of the gentlemen from the Orient. The New York State Assembly, pressed by the State Chamber of Commerce, finally passed a Midland aid bill which would have added about one million dollars to the Midland coffers. An indication that this help was necessary was the complete suspension of work on the DeRuyter line.

# NEW YORK AND OSWEGO
# MIDLAND RAILROAD,
### BETWEEN
## LAKE ONTARIO AND THE ATLANTIC.

**Two Express Trains daily each way, with Luxurious Day and Night Cars attached, run between New York and Oswego without change.**

## ARRANGEMENT OF THROUGH PASSENGER TRAINS.

| WESTWARD. | | | | EASTWARD. | | | |
|---|---|---|---|---|---|---|---|
| *STATIONS.* | No. 2. Through Mail. | No. 4. Ontario Exp. | | *STATIONS.* | No. 1. Through Mail. | No. 3. Atlantic Exp. | |
| New York..................Leave | 7.50 A. M. | 6.30 P. M. | | Oswego ......................Leave | 7.00 A. M. | 6.00 P. M. | |
| Jersey City...... .......... " | 8.00 " | 6.40 " | | Fulton.................... " | 7.28 " | 6.25 " | |
| Hackensack.................. " | 8.52 " | 6.40 " | | Central Square............... " | 7.58 " | 6.55 " | |
| Paterson............. ....... " | 9.12 " | 7.01 " | | Cleveland............. " | 8.30 " | 7.25 " | |
| Newark....................... " | 8.35 " | 6.25 " | | Oneida...... ................. " | 9.20 " | 8.00 " | |
| Montclair..................... " | 8.55 " | 6.39 " | | Eaton...................... " | 10.10 " | | |
| Newfoundland.... ..... .... " | 10.29 " | 8.24 " | | Utica....................... " | 7.25 " | 5.15 " | |
| Franklin....... ..... .... .... " | 11.06 " | 8.54 " | | Rome....................... " | 7.00 " | 4.50 " | |
| Unionville................... " | 11.47 " | 9.36 " | | Cortland..................... " | 9.00 " | 3.00 " | |
| Middletown .................. " | 12.38 P.M. | 10.12 " | | Norwich............. .......... " | 11.12 " | 9.30 " | |
| Ellenville...................Arrive | 1.50 " | | | Oxford...... ............. ...... " | 11.35 " | 9.55 " | |
| Liberty....................Leave | 2.31 " | 11.58 " | | New Berlin.................. " | 10.25 " | | |
| Hancock.................... " | 4.11 " | 1.38 A. M. | | Sidney...................... " | 12.17 P. M. | 10.44 " | |
| Walton........................ " | 4.55 " | 2.20 " | | Delhi ...................... " | 12.10 " | | |
| Delhi ..... ................Arrive | 9.35 " | 8.00 " | | Walton....................... " | 1.17 " | 11.48 " | |
| Sidney....................Leave | 5.52 " | 3.16 " | | Hancock..................... " | 1.58 " | 12.36 A. M. | |
| New Berlin ..... ...........Arrive | 7.20 " | 9.05 " | | Liberty...................... " | 3.44 " | 2.22 " | |
| Oxford...................Leave | 6.32 " | 3.58 " | | Ellenville...................... " | 4.00 " | | |
| Norwich.................... " | 7.10 " | 4.20 " | | Middletown ...................... " | 5.36 " | 4.10 " | |
| Cortland..........Arrive | 9.40 " | | | Unionville...................... " | 6.17 " | 4.47 " | |
| Rome....................... " | 10.15 " | 12.05 P. M. | | Franklin................. ........... " | 7.00 " | 5.22 " | |
| Utica.......................... " | 9.55 " | 11.10 A. M. | | Newfoundland..... ......... " | 7.38 " | 6.00 " | |
| Eaton................. .........Leave | 8.14 " | 5.22 " | | Montclair ...... ............ " | | 7.34 " | |
| Oneida............. ...... ... " | 9.00 " | 6.10 " | | Newark...................... " | | 7.47 " | |
| Cleveland................... " | 9.39 " | 6.40 " | | Paterson...................Arrive | 8.50 " | 7.46 " | |
| Central Square............... " | 10.14 " | 7.03 " | | Hackensack...... ............. " | 9.09 " | 8.09 " | |
| Fulton........................ " | 10.47 " | 7.28 " | | Jersey City ...................... " | 9.47 ,, | 7.41 " | |
| Oswego......................Arrive | 11.15 P. M. | 7.55 A. M. | | New York..................... " | 10.00 P. M. | 7.50 A. M. | |

## The only Daily Line between New York and Oswego.

Excursion Tickets to New York and return, good until October 1st, 1873, on Sale at all Ticket Stations West of Liberty, at a reduction of 25 per cent. from Regular Rates.

### Ask for a New York Excursion Ticket via this New, Short and Picturesque Route.
#### Quick Time and Sure Connections. Baggage Checked Through.
*Passenger Depots in New York, foot of Courtlandt and Desbrosses Streets, and Jersey City.*
##### GENERAL OFFICES, III LIBERTY STREET, NEW YORK.

*Gerald M. Best*

In 1873 the New Jersey Midland and the Middletown, Unionville and Water Gap formed the southern link for the Oswego Midland.

When Governor Hoffman vetoed the aid bill, doubts arose as to the ability of the company to meet its financial obligations. Sporadic labor troubles broke out all along the line, largely controlled in the fashion of the time—the men were fired, often without collecting their pay. The state did attempt to relieve the Midland money pinch by amending the Town Bonding Act to permit savings banks to invest in the venture. However, the legislature was now exhibiting the slightest amount of caution, much overdue, about the Midland. It added a stipulation that county treasurers must maintain a sinking fund for redemption of the town bonds.

The year 1871 saw continued activity in the Midland country. The Ellenville branch and a section twenty-seven miles long, from Middletown to Centerville (divided by the unfinished Shawangunk tunnel) were opened. Nevertheless, the hesitancy of the railroad to run trains over the just-completed DeRuyter line hinted that the construction was not of the best quality. They appeared to be observing the dictum that "haste makes waste." Also, the great tunnel was a source of frustration. All during the spring the rock in the west end of the bore took on a malevolent personality all its own. Without warning, sections of the floor began to collapse and blow up, throwing stunned and bewildered men in all directions. Landslides occurring almost daily held up trains on the completed track between Morrisville and Eaton.

Less ambitious men might have taken these portents rather seriously, but the projectors of the Midland found encouragement in the reports that gold-bearing quartz had been discovered in the Shawangunk tunnel—possibly enough to finish the line without the state aid that had been denied them. This dream, like so many other Midland dreams, had no substance. Ironically, the Legislature, still under the enchantment of Littlejohn and Low, passed an enabling bill permitting the company to extend its trackage "to any point on Lake Erie or the Niagara River." Without the ring of hard cash, this seemed an empty gesture, like a warm handshake for a hungry man. No worries seemed to cloud the imagination of the Midland managers, for they now began investigation of a *brand-new* main line from Hancock straight to Cortland and beyond. And President Littlejohn went ahead with a lease of the Middletown & Crawford for 99 years, in order to obtain right-of-way north out of Middletown. Corporate bonds with the New Jersey Midland were also strengthened.

The corporate overlap of the New York and Oswego Midland with the New Jersey Midland could not have been clearer than when engine *No. 2* of the Jersey line was delivered in April of 1871 with the name "C. A. Wortendyke" emblazoned on the cab. *No. 1* was unnamed, but obviously had been reserved for a tribute to Littlejohn. A few of these first locomotives on the NJM were lettered "New York Midland," a blow to New Jersey pride, but suggestive of the merger which never materialized. The little Middletown, Unionville & Water Gap Railroad was grafted onto the Oswego Midland to achieve a junction between these two larger roads near Franklin, New Jersey. With such elaborate preparations made, it might be thought that Dame Fortune smiled down upon the venture. Such was not the case, however.

Hard luck hounded the Midland. Oswego citizens eyed the DeRuyter branch with some apprehension, for their claim to greatness for this Great Lakes port depended, to a large extent, on becoming the northern terminus of the line out of New York City. The public announcement of the project to take the main line from Hancock to Cortland met with understandable resistance from Oswego as well as from all other communities north of Hancock, and the plan was promptly forgotten. The Erie Railroad, the largest taxpayer in the town of Hancock, began agitating for the repudiation of the town bonds. Residents of Hancock shared this sentiment and carried their case to court, where they lost but established a precedent that was to be followed by other governmental bodies along the route in years to come. Even the completion of the Blooming-burg tunnel could not calm the fears of investors.

At Bloomingburg the removal of 61,600 yards of rock from the tunnel of 3,850 feet was completed on October 19, 1871, after a long period of around-the-clock digging. The annoyed inhabitants of by-passed Monticello had made this enterprise into the bugbear of the entire construction. They claimed that the resources of the company would be drained by this enor-mous project and that either the bore would never be com-pleted or the railroad would go into early bankruptcy and fail of its original purpose. The worthies of this lovely village felt that they were fighting for their economic life, and to counteract the effect of the new railroad's five-mile distance from Monticello, they organized the line named the Monticello & Port Jervis Company. Despite such public alarms, the work went on. The supervisor for the tunnel excavation was well selected. Anthony Jones, who later worked with the Northern Pacific Railroad Company, pushed his crews forward from both ends of the mountain, with a show of outward confidence. He would have been justified in having some private doubts, for the circum-stances which made this tunnel unusual and difficult were a six-hundred-foot curve from the east and a double incline. An engineer who directed his digging teams past each other would have sealed his fate in the profession forever. The error in joining the two sections was less than one inch—a tribute to the care and ability of this young man.

The most prized souvenir of the Shawangunk tunnel con-struction was the last drill—the tool which would make the first perforation. Late in September of 1871 sounds from the east told the western team that the drill would soon appear on their side. They slackened off until the point of the boring tool appeared. Rough hands seized it, wedged it with a pick axe and pulled it through. Then, with great haste, they buried it under three or four tons of rock, placing another drill on the floor in the meantime. This substitute drill was taken with

*page* 22

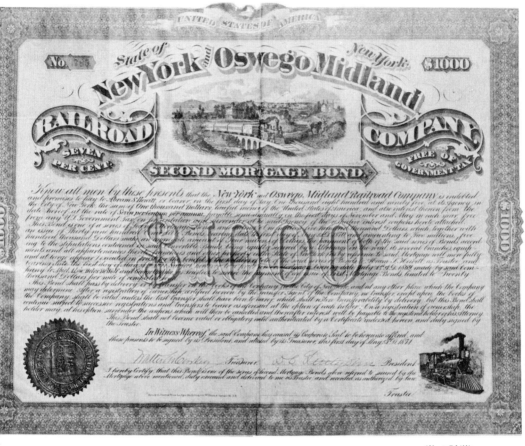

Impressively ornate, the tax-free bond belonged to Abram S. Hewitt, soon to be called upon to rescue his investment.

much ceremony to the local blacksmith's shop where it was cut up for exhibition purposes. Mr. J. V. Morrison, who perpetrated the hoax, revealed it later and sent the stolen relic on to Albany. The first man through the passage was the eminent Henry R. Low, and the first train puffed gently into the inner recesses of the Shawangunk tunnel on January 24, 1872.

In spite of discouragements and disappointments, the Midland was now substantially complete. It connected with the Albany & Susquehanna (Delaware and Hudson) at Sidney Plains; with the Erie at Middletown; with the Delaware, Lackawanna & Western at Norwich; with the Utica & Black River at Utica; with the Rome, Watertown & Ogdensburg at Rome; with the Syracuse & Chenango Valley at Earlville; with the Cazenovia & Canastota at DeRuyter. At least thirty-three engines were running and twenty-eight more were on order. The road was still running in disconnected sections, with an unfinished portion in Delaware County. The earnings, although up from preceding years, were insufficient in 1872 to meet the interest on the bonds.

The Auburn Branch (the grander name for the DeRuyter line) had opened on July 26, 1871 with a passenger train from Norwich drawn by locomotive *No. 15*, the *DeRuyter,* with Emery Card as engineer and David Shattuck, conductor. This wandering iron trail was built by way of diminutive settlements distinguished from the surrounding fields and hills by such names as South Plymouth, Plymouth, Ireland's Mills, Beaver Meadow, Otselic Center and Crumb Hill. Hard-working sons of Erin had pecked out the dirt for two-wheeled mule carts, which carried their earthen loads off to build new embankments. Narrow-gauge gravity cars were also employed to carry badly needed fill down to the construction sites. When the crews reached DeRuyter they made a sharp right-angle turn to the south and hooked up to the Ithaca & Cortland, which granted Midland trackage rights. Then they struck out from Freeville at another right angle, roughly paralleling the Southern Central (Lehigh Valley) toward Auburn. When the rails reached Venice, observers were strengthened in their belief that the rails would eventually lead to the shores of Erie.

On December 16, 1872, through passenger service to Scipio Center was instituted, with a stage company supplying the transportation into Auburn. Unfortunately, there were almost no paying customers, except for occasional special excursions, after the initial trip. Perhaps only the train crews could put up with the infernal screeching of the dried-out timber trestles. Several of these slender wooden bridges had been raised to cross great gaps too high and wide for immediate filling. The structure at Wilbert's farm was the highest (95 feet) and the "Rainbow" at Otselic Center the longest (700 feet).

At the operating level there were strange occurrences. The lack of a telegraph system led to embarrassing situations. On one trip, a train from Norwich arrived at Smith's Valley (Randallsville) ten minutes behind time and took the siding for the down train. One hour passed rather quickly. By the end of the second, however, the streams of tobacco juice from the engine cab came more explosively and the tact of the conductor was giving way to irritation. When the third hour had passed, the harassed ticket-puncher could take no more complaints from his angry passengers. He mounted a borrowed horse and jogged down the line to locate the trouble. At Hamilton he discovered the down train three hours late, too, waiting for the up train. A railroad run on such a schedule could not hope to compete with the established stage lines.

Shortly thereafter, three hundred strikers quit construction work on the Midland and marched up the line from Hancock almost to Walton, gathering strength as they went. Soon their anger dissipated, in direct ratio to the number of miles traveled, and they dropped out a few at a time until none were left with stamina to continue. A spark-spouting locomotive set a destructive fire south of Ellenville that raged out of control for days. A relatively minor accident claimed the life of Milo H.

The carpenter's dream near Otselic Center was nicknamed the "Rainbow Trestle" because of its height and crescent-shaped curve.

| N. Y. & OSWEGO MIDLAND R. R. **DE RUYTER** TO **NEWARK.** Not good unless stamped by Ticket Agent. | N. Y. & OSWEGO MIDLAND R. R. **UTICA** TO **PLYMOUTH.** Not good unless stamped by Ticket Agent. |
|---|---|

Two passenger tickets list stations on lines abandoned (DeRuyter and Plymouth) and shunned (Newark, on the NJM).

Tift on Randall's work train out of Oneida—the first train crewman to die at his post. He had applied the tender brakes while the engine was backing up, and when the train derailed, he was thrown into the mud beneath the overturned locomotive. In July, 1872, at nearly the same spot, a freight train jumped the tracks, smashing eight or nine cars and delaying passenger traffic for many hours. A new depot and most of a standing train of new passenger coaches went up in smoke at Delhi soon after.

Tunnel explosions, derailments, disastrous fires, landslides, bridge collapses and similar phenomena were characteristic of nineteenth century railroading and must not be viewed as unique to the Midland. These were part of the normal risk of building and running a railway.

On January 1st of 1873 the Montclair branch of the New Jersey Midland was operating trains from Cortlandt Street to Ringwood and Monks, a distance of 38½ miles. The gap in Delaware County was rapidly being closed and final arrangements were being made to lease the Utica and Rome companies.

Qualms felt by Midland investors were not shared by the laboring men. The attractiveness of the new railroad drew so many determined job applicants that Superintendent W. P. McKinley was forced to publish a general notice that persons offering bribes to get conductor's positions would be prosecuted unless such applications ceased. The stockholders were hardly so optimistic; they watched the estimated cost of construction rise from $10,000 a mile in 1866 to $40,000 a mile in 1872 to $80,000 a mile in 1873. But there had been substantial progress. The annual report issued in April of 1873 listed 84 locomotives; 51 passenger coaches; 30 baggage, mail and express cars; 359 box and stock cars; 609 flat cars; 17 cabooses; 400 gondolas; 96 gravel and ore cars; 196 four-wheeled coal cars and six snow plows. The New Jersey Midland, including the Montclair Railway, was transferred by lease to the Oswego Midland in June of 1872. The Montclair had evidently been the favored route into New Jersey, but engineering and financial barriers stood in the way of its completion. Its rails ended at Greenwood Lake on the state line and it was never extended through Sugar Loaf into Middletown. When OM trains rattled south towards New York City, the Montclair was used as an alternate route from Pompton Junction only. Even those who might defend the steep cost of the Midland construction would have blanched at the outlay for this "short-cut"—$200,000 per mile.

The new snowplows got their first workout early in March when a wild snowstorm hit upstate New York and filled Walker's Cut, between Higginsville and Fish Creek. One shining plow coupled to three snorting locomotives made a gallant effort to knock a hole in this drifted white wall. The sole result of the assault was a bone-shaking stop which dumped wood from the engine tenders onto the crews.

On the 24th of May the company itself struck a financial obstacle. The money was running out and no more was forthcoming. Spurning his gift for turning a fine phrase, President Littlejohn submitted a rather commonplace resignation. George Opdyke took control and glossed over the current troubles with an eloquent speech about the imminent "breakthrough" to Buffalo and Lake Erie. Littlejohn stepped down to vice-president and took charge of this "Western Extension." To bolster their tottering empire, these men could report the first through train from Oswego to Jersey City on July 10, 1873. The evening before, the last rail had been spiked down twelve miles west of Westfield Flats (Roscoe). The west rail, about twelve feet long, was engraved with the name "D. C. Littlejohn," the east rail with "George Opdyke." Elisha P. Wheeler, former vice-president, was called upon to drive the last spike. Hatless and stripped to the waist, he hammered it into place with an exact (and a prophetic) thirteen strokes. Thus, at 8:15 p.m. on a cloudy and overcast day, in the middle of nowhere, to the accompaniment of five locomotive whistles, the inevitable cannon fire and the halting strains of the local musical aggregation, the New York and Oswego Midland became a reality. Only one major figure was unable to be present. Dewitt C. Littlejohn had urgent business elsewhere.

When a permanent lease of the New Jersey Midland was announced in September, the OM was obliged to shoulder an even bigger financial burden. The terms included the payment of a floating debt of $265,000 and rental of $1,500 a day for the first ten days and $2,000 a day thereafter, until all NJM debts were paid.

The staggering costs incurred by the new railroad could be borne no longer. The Panic of 1873 was simply an added blow to the fallen corporation, and bankruptcy came almost as a blessing. As the affairs of the New York and Oswego Midland moved inevitably into the courts, Dewitt C. Littlejohn receded quietly into the background. A sudden interest in lumbering took him out of the city of Oswego into the timber lands. He would never "railroad" again.

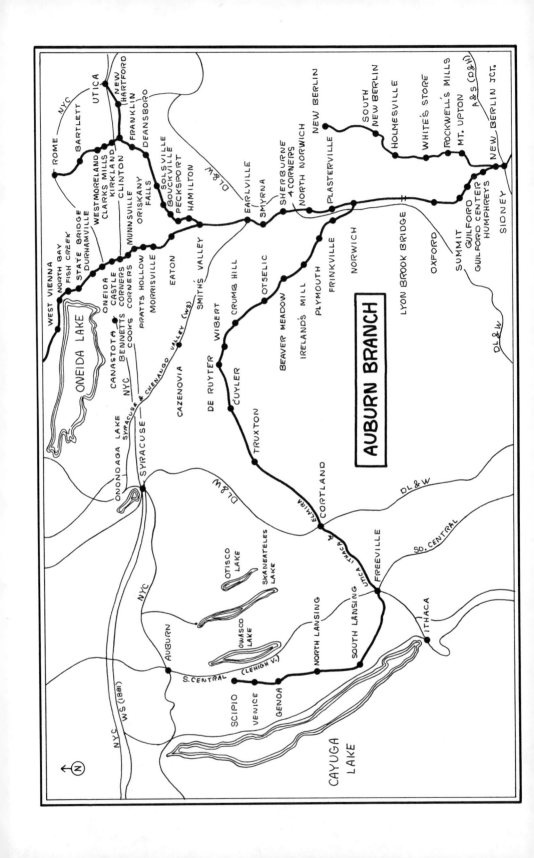

CHAPTER TWO

W HEN IT ENTERED receivership
in July of 1873, the Oswego
Midland consisted of a rambling stretch of rails dodging through
the hills and over the valleys of some of the roughest territory
in New York State. The final survey line had been set not so
much according to the best natural route nor consistent with
the location of the major industrial cities; it had been kinked
and twisted to pass through those communities which had provided the necessary funds for its construction. Provisions for
keeping the railroad alive after its birth were never made.
Puzzled outsiders might easily remark, "It's pretty, but what's
it for?"

The two men selected to save the railroad from complete
ruin were Abram S. Hewitt and James G. Stevens. Nothing
could be achieved by grumbling about the line of rails itself,
so the receivers looked to see what they had to work with.
Ninety-four first-class locomotives made an impressive roster,
even if the list fell six short of the planned one hundred. The
*Oakland* and five others never saw Midland service. The *Oakland* was orphaned in this fashion: as *No. 89*, she had been
ordered, built and lettered, but a mechanical flaw developed
which was not corrected until after the Midland bankruptcy.
Therefore, the Rhode Island Company leased her to the Boston
& Providence and later sold her to the Providence & Worcester
as their *Columbus.*

Two more engines were eliminated from the active service
in a quite different fashion. September 26 promised to be a

Abram S. Hewitt was a shrewd and able administrator charged with the
duty of rejuvenating the railroad old beyond its years.

chilly, overcast day, and the morning sun was unable to pierce the heavy fog that hung low along the railroad embankment on the Jersey shore of the Hudson. Conductor Gilbert's way freight chugged out of the Jersey City terminal at 4:10 a.m., about one hour late. Rumbling north through the clouds of mist, it halted for orders at West End two hours and twenty minutes later. Although he was instructed to wait in the clear for the southbound local passenger just steaming out of Wortendyke, Gilbert consulted his watch and decided to run for Homestead. Had he checked his timepiece with the station clock, Gilbert would have discovered an error of eight minutes in favor of the passenger train. Gambling on eight minutes he did not have, the conductor waved his engineer a highball and swung aboard. Just short of safety, the slight miscalculation became the steel certainties of engines 58 and 36 pilot to pilot. With a thunderous crash, both engines rose into the air like fighting stallions and fell together. Three men died in the disaster: Kelly, the passenger engineer; Messener, the freight fireman and McNeil, a station hand.

Effects of the Midland bankruptcy were felt everywhere. The layoff of hundreds of workmen at the Rogers Locomotive Works was blamed on the Midland, although this claim was exaggerated. Irate stockholders fumed and discontented employees rebelled. Some few people could be philosophical, even humorous, despite the calamity. One official received an investor's telegram which begged that the investor's interests be protected. The reply read:

> How can I save others when myself I cannot save? Beyond this roaring flood are pleasant fields and pastures green. Read good books and abstain from profanity.

Hewitt and Stevens had walked into a hornet's nest. In November unpaid wages amounted to $459,000, and expenses exceeded receipts by approximately $3,000 a day. In addition, the Middletown shops, an absolute necessity, were under construction (on land purchased from the Midland's Henry R.

Low), requiring considerable financial outlay. A voter's referendum in Hancock, New York, resulted in a 335 to 2 decision to resist further payment on its bonds. Auburn waxed indignant over the reduction of trains to three per week, with rumored winter suspension. To top it all off, mail trains 1 and 2 slammed into each other near Hancock because of faulty train orders. When shipping arrangements with the now-independent New Jersey Midland became difficult, only courageous or foolhardy men could hope for the company's future. The Montclair line, to which the Oswego Midland held title, was not only inaccessible but so skimpily built that it was not suitable for through traffic anyway. Without any outward evidence of disenchantment, the managers contracted with the Erie for transfer of freight and passengers to the older company's broad gauge cars at Middletown. Further negotiations with the New Jersey Midland resulted in a new transfer agreement, in return for which the NJM obtained badly needed rolling stock for its own operation. And the Montclair Railway (called an "unprofitable siding" by critics) passed out of OM hands when the Chancellor of New Jersey auctioned it off to satisfy right-of-way claims against it.

As soon as his duties permitted, Receiver Stevens conducted the first objective inspection of the railroad. This report, dated 1874, was thorough and honest. The 56-pound rail he found to be "of good quality and in fair condition, excepting that laid between Oxford and Eaton," which was giving out rapidly. The hemlock ties and trestles were "decaying fast" and "needed heavy repair." Because the cuts had been dug in the easiest and fastest way possible, landslides were constantly occurring, delaying trains for long periods. The glamor was stripped from Littlejohn's eloquent descriptions of the main line in Stevens' direct prose:

> From Oneida north the increase of traffic will be slow; the soil is generally poor, the towns small, and nothing that at present can be seen warrants any hope of rapid growth in the future.

At last the company had a man who could see with open eyes that light traffic, a poor roadbed, inadequate bridges and featherweight rails did not add up to a first class railroad.

Nor would men work without wages. Groups of workers chained down locomotives, spiked switches and tore up the track at Walton, Summitville and other points along the line as a protest against the lack of payment. When the engineers threatened to walk out, Hewitt stated:

> Assure the engineers for me personally that there is not a dollar in the possession of the receivers to meet the back payroll. If they choose to stop the road, they can do so (and lose all chance of getting it) . . .

Periodically, new outbreaks of employee violence disturbed the management, but these were relatively mild compared with the assaults made on the Midland by the outraged communities which had been "cheated" by the bankruptcy.

Tax collectors up and down the line swooped down on railroad equipment. At Delhi, a loaded passenger train was stopped and impounded. At DeRuyter, a passenger coach and four box cars were seized. At New Berlin, a locomotive was chained and padlocked. At Smith's Valley, twenty-four freight cars were claimed. Unsatisfied tax bills gave countless hamlets revenge for their financial losses. In spite of a court injunction restraining towns from selling this equipment, it stayed in their possession and operations became very risky. Conditions were so bad that Hewitt released a public notice that if tax collectors continued to seize rolling stock, the railroad would close down completely.

Passenger service in many areas was reduced to a single coach in fading maroon livery trailing a slow freight train. A mail train was delayed twenty-seven hours at Cooks Falls when it was entrapped in a mud slide. Abandonment of the entire road was advocated by more than one observer, and the *Syracuse Standard* printed a sarcastic news item which pointedly fixed the blame for the Midland's predicament:

Honorable D. C. Littlejohn has been elected a Fellow of the American Geographical Society of New York. That is a deserved honor. No man in the state knows anything like as much about the geography of central New York as the Honorable D. C. He has canvassed it, surveyed it, stumped it, built a very crooked railroad all over it, and finally persuaded the simple natives to mortgage it. Why shouldn't he be elected a fellow?

Disregarding the more extreme critics, Hewitt and Stevens kept going as best they could, even improving the property where there was need for improvement. But these patching projects were also unlucky. On the 24th of October near Trout Brook, Engineer Moore's work train was working the south side of the switch, and another work train driven by Bill McCloud was busy to the north. When the time approached for the arrival of the regular freight train, both engineers returned to the siding. McCloud was able to clear the main line, but Moore took more time and sent his flagman up the track north of the switch. The engineer of the approaching freight waved to the flagman, assuming that he belonged to the only train visible to him—McCloud's, which was safely off the main line. He opened the throttle another notch and his train picked up speed again. In a few moments he came up against Moore's standing train and rammed him before he could apply the brakes. One life was lost—G. Hoffenburger, fireman of the work train. The location of the collision is noteworthy; it occurred within yards of the site where the last rail was laid.

Finally, the situation became too much for the receivers to bear, and at midnight, February 27, 1875, the Midland ceased operating by order of Messrs. Hewitt and Stevens. The D&H Canal Company (which operated the Albany and Susquehanna) stepped in to run trains from Sidney to Utica and Rome, but the remainder of the railroad was abandoned. Assuming that his purchase agreement with the OM would not be lived up to, a farmer named Bennett at Westfield Flats tore up the rails across his farm and plowed down the roadbed. A Mrs. Porter of New Hurley was arrested a month later for repeatedly ripping up the tracks with the aid of an axe and a 15-year-old son. She fought off an engine crew with stones and could not be mollified until she was taken before Federal Judge Blatchford in New York City. He assured her that she would keep her rights to payment for her land. The suspension of operations continued for better than thirty days, and was resumed with only such interruptions as indignant land-owners like these provided. In the fall of this same year, impounded equipment was actually auctioned off by tax collectors and apparently sold back to company bidders.

The length of track between Trout Brook and Westfield Flats was again the scene of an accident when a snowplow and its locomotive left the rails on February 2, 1876. Riding the engine was Superintendent Henry M. Flint, and Master Mechanic John Minshull was aboard the plow. The engineman was the same William McCloud who had been a horrified witness to the recent Trout Brook accident. Caroming off the side of a bridge over the Beaver Kill, the plow and engine plunged headlong into the stream, carrying most of the bridge supports with them. Flint was pinned next to the boiler head, surrounded by escaping steam. While other crew members pried the unfortunate man out of his own private Hell, Minshull stumbled up the embankment to flag the following mail train. Ironically, the nearest shelter to the accident scene was the frame farmhouse of the same Mr. Bennett who had ripped up the tracks across his property. Nevertheless, Bennett provided what small comfort he could for a suffering fellow human, and there Flint died of his terrible injuries.

In spite of bankruptcy, accidents, tax collectors, strikes and sundry minor disturbances, business for the OM was picking up. The milk traffic, which had started in 1871 as a single car on a passenger train from Bloomingburg to Middletown (eight miles), where the cans were transferred to the broad gauge Erie, increased to 900 cans per day, with the run extended to

Liberty. The Philadelphia Centennial promised to add to railroad coffers many extra passenger fares. The Midland advertised a special fleet of twelve-wheeled coaches, painted a glistening white, equipped with colored porters, "to be occupied as homes both night and day." Although Hewitt discouraged the naming of locomotives, one was refurbished at Middletown and named *Henry M. Flint* to immortalize the late superintendent and to power Centennial trains. Plans were laid for a strawberry train to run on a fast schedule between Oswego and New York.

The black sheep of the Midland line was the section of rural trackage which meandered almost aimlessly in the general direction of Buffalo. To add to the management's chagrin at the paltry receipts from Auburn Branch traffic, the citizenry was becoming most difficult. A dispute between a tax collector's aides and Midland employees resulted in gains for both sides in the form of blackened eyes, bloodied noses, and mutual legal processes. Cuyler, which was the center of resistance, had refused to sign company-sponsored petitions to the Legislature for remission of property taxes. Soon no trains stopped at Cuyler depot, but these resolute farmers refused to submit to Midland terms. In June of 1876, on a single occasion, the regular train made a stop at Cuyler. The choice was not that of the train crew; it was the natural consequence of jamming into a huge barrier of stones, timbers, and rails erected just east of the station. A compromise was finally effected, for no town could hold its head high when its depot stood locked and vacant, and while its passengers were forced to drive to a neighboring train stop. Understandably enough, hard feelings persisted on both sides.

The scheduling of the Centennial trains was a profitable move, and numerous York-Staters took advantage of low rates and commodious accommodations. Section after section of renovated coaches moved southward over the OM, the NJM and the Pennsylvania to prepared side tracks near the exhibition grounds. The extra traffic burden also brought operating dangers, which became manifest on the late evening of October

23, 1876. Section 2 of a Centennial special paused briefly at Sandburgh by order of Superintendent Tom Purdy, who was personally overseeing the operation from one of the coaches. The flagman was then called in and the train started. Suddenly, the brakes were applied again in response to two rings on the signal bell. Before the bewildered flagman could hit the cinders once more, Section 3 slid, brakes screeching, into the rear coach of the standing cars. One unlucky passenger standing on the rear platform for some fresh air seemed hypnotized by the white eye of the approaching headlamp. He remained in this perilous position until the life was crushed out of him by the colliding locomotive. The engineer of Section 3, Ed McNiff, was more fortunate; he escaped unscathed from the wreckage of the crumpled cab and splintered coach.

The mystery of the second disastrous stop at Sandburgh was never solved; the hand on the signal cord was never identified. The superstitious could point meaningfully at this incident, at the many wrecks near Westfield Flats, at the financial difficulties and last of all, to an eerie experience near Walton. Piloting an evening train through a late summer thunderstorm, Engineer Cal Sanford found himself assaulted by wind, rain and hail. The surrounding hills echoed the frequent peals of thunder. Lightning streaked through the skies. These rendered the laboring locomotive noises almost soundless and the combined headlamp and firebox glow nearly unnoticeable. One brilliant yellow bolt fastened itself momentarily onto the smokestack, enveloping the engine in a sheet of blinding flame. Sanford shut off steam and stared in horror as his driving wheels turned into a fireworks display—iron pinwheels throwing off multi-colored sparks. The phenomenon lasted but a few moments; the shaken engine crew would never forget it.

These lean years had taught the railroad how to exist on a minimum of expenditure. Locomotive equipment now commonly included broad-axes and cross-cut saws as standard equipment, in order that engine fuel would always be available

*No. 2* blocked a rural highway to show off its shining brass and gilt lettering. Engineer Pat Fogarty stands in the gangway.

*No. 3,* the *Chenango,* stops for water and a portrait of train crew and passengers.

In the days when mustaches were things of beauty,
Cal Sanford's "walrus" was a standout.

*Harry Sanford*

At the end of the Delhi run, *No. 76* served as background for a picture of Bill Root, trainman;
Cal Sanford, engineer; Bill Foster, fireman and "Windy" Norton, watchman.

*Robert F. Harding*

from along the right-of-way. The smaller depots stared with vacant eyes at the infrequent passing trains. Having learned that a railroad without a telegraph could lead to a regular posse of mounted conductors, the managers solved its communications problem in a most ingenious way. One of the solutions was Charles H. Crockett, a qualified telegraph operator, assigned to passenger runs as a flagman. The protection he afforded his train was rather unusual. At each specified unoccupied depot, the train halted to permit Crockett to run for the station, unlock the door, plug in his portable telegraph key and receive orders from the dispatcher. The delay was not great and traffic was speeded greatly by this innovation.

Although Fate may have set her hand against the enterprise, the faith of many citizens remained unshaken. The village of Ellenville raised $1,000 of a $1,400 tax bill in order to restore train service on their branch. The blunt Hewitt pursued a policy of discontinuing service to communities which placed too great a tax burden on the railroad. When the great railroad insurrection of 1877 occurred, it found the Midland employees loyal and contented for the first time since the commencement of operations. The pay car had been rolling up and down the line with unbelievable regularity, and the railroad from Oswego was the only one making regular milk deliveries in New York City.

The only drawback to this tale of improving Midland fortunes was the spur to DeRuyter and beyond. The *DeRuyter Gleaner* noted the passing of a steam-propelled car (inspection car #3) in October of 1878, and this inspection trip would be the last before the branch line, variously called the Western Extension, the Auburn Branch, and the DeRuyter Line, would literally be "snowed under." After a heavy snowfall had blocked off all train movements to the west, the OM management completely abandoned the many-trestled outlet "to the shores of the Erie." Except for a fabulous gravity (downgrade to Norwich) and horse (return to Beaver Meadow) train "driven"

DeForest Douglas Diver Collection of Railroad Photographs,
Cornell University, Collection of Regional History,
courtesy S. O. Kimball

Inspection engine #3 had a roomy leather front seat, from which Master Mechanic Minshull leapt to his death.

This blind crossing at Trout Brook was the scene of the wagon-inspection engine wreck of 1879.

D. Diver Collection at Cornell, courtesy S. O. Kimball

IN MEMORY OF
JOHN E. MINSHULL
MASTER MECHANIC
OF THE N.Y. AND OSWEGO
MIDLAND R.R.
BORN SEPT. 19, 1849.
DIED AUG. 19, 1879.

ERECTED BY HIS FELLOW
OFFICERS AND LABORERS
AS AN EXPRESSION OF THEIR
REGARD FOR THE MANLINESS,
INTEGRITY AND GENEROSITY
OF HIS CHARACTER, AND OF
THEIR DEEP AFFECTION FOR
ONE WHOSE AIM IT WAS TO
KNOW AND DO THE RIGHT.

*D. Diver Collection at Cornell, courtesy S. O. Kimball*

The loss of the Midland's young master mechanic was keenly felt by all.

by an enterprising lumber dealer, Thurlow Johnson, and a home-made steam car piloted by Milo Miles, the rails were left to rust and weeds. Only the portion from DeRuyter to Freeville would survive, as a section of the Utica, Ithaca & Elmira (Lehigh Valley).

Personal misfortune was responsible for the fastest time on the new Delhi branch, which was never to be equalled again, made by engine #21 running light, with Cal Sanford at the throttle. On October 13, 1878, Sanford, who came to the Midland from the Rome, Watertown & Ogdensburgh, had arrived at Walton on his regular run, to be notified that his wife was near death in Delhi. He quickly received authorization to uncouple from his train and run to Delhi without speed restrictions. The sad journey was made in seventeen minutes—an average of 60 miles per hour.

The last days of the Midland were at hand. The road had been up for sale for about two years, and the vastly improved balance sheets would not go unnoticed for long. The strict economies practiced by her court-appointed managers had turned the trick. For instance, the new owners of the railway would find a large stable of disabled iron horses in Middletown, sacrificed to Hewitt's policy of "Replace—don't repair." With a low traffic density and an abundance of motive power, the Midland could afford to "hammer" its engines until they came apart, but the spares had now run out. True to its old hard-luck days, just as a competent motive power specialist was needed, Master Mechanic Minshull was killed as he jumped from the forward seat of inspection car #3 before it struck a log-laden wagon at a country crossing.

By November of 1879, rumors spread along Wall Street, on up the Midland main line, eventually to the farthest reaches of OM iron. Hope, destroyed by bankruptcy a few years before, was resurrected. There was still time for the Midland to become the "Grand Trunk Line" its promoters had promised. New blood, new money, and new life were forthcoming.

# New York, West Shore & Buffalo Railway Company

## AND

# New York, Ontario & Western Railway Co.

## JOINT TIME TABLE No. 1.

### TO TAKE EFFECT MONDAY, JUNE 4, 1883.

*(Superseding N. Y., O. & W. R'way Time Table No. 10.)*

## MAIN LINE AND BRANCHES.

☛ Trains are run by New York time. This Time Table will not be used upon the N. Y., S. & W. R. R. or upon the Penna. R. R.

| New York, West Shore and Buffalo Railway. | New York, Ontario and Western Railway. |
|---|---|
| J. E. CHILDS, Asst. General Superintendent. | J. E. CHILDS, Gen'l Superintendent. |
| E. CANFIELD, Acting Division Superintendent. | C. W. LANPHER, Supt. Northern Division. |
| | N. R. HANKINS, "  Middle  " |
| | E. CANFIELD, "  Southern  " |

*Gerald M. Best*

Under joint operation, the O&W had three divisions: the Northern (Oswego to Norwich), Middle (Norwich to Middletown) and Southern (Middletown to Weehawken).

*page 46*

# STATION TELEGRAPH CALLS
# NEW YORK, ONTARIO & WESTERN RAILWAY

## SOUTHERN DIVISION

|  |  |
| --- | --- |
| New York | GS |
| Weehawken, N.J. | W |
| Cornwall, N.Y. | CW |
| Firthcliffe | MX |
| Meadow Brook | MW |
| Little Britian | GN |
| Burnside | BS |
| Burnside Tower | RX |
| Campbell Hall | CH |
| Campbell Hall (Erie Crossing) | MQ |
| Crystal Run | ID |
| Middletown | MD |
| Middletown Yard | AV |
| Crawford Junction | RF |
| Bloomingburgh | BH |
| Mamakating | WU |
| Summitville | SV |
| Mountain Dale | UN |
| Woodridge | CI |
| Fallsburgh | FG |
| Luzon | HY |
| Ferndale | FA |
| Liberty | RY |
| Parksville | PE |
| Livingston Manor | VN |
| Roscoe | RK |
| Cooks Falls | CF |
| Horton | HN |
| Trout Brook | BK |
| East Branch | BC |
| Fish's Eddy | CF |
| Cadosia | HD |
| Apex | XY |
| Rock Rift | RO |
| Beerston | RS |
| Walton | WN |
| Northfield | ZA |
| Merrickville | MK |
| Franklin | FE |
| Maywood | SC |
| Youngs | YO |
| South Unadilla | UD |
| Sidney | SI |

## PORT JERVIS, MONTICELLO and KINGSTON BRANCHES

|  |  |
| --- | --- |
| Monticello | MO |
| St. Joseph's | SJ |
| Valley Junction | VJ |
| Wurtsboro | WB |
| Summitville | SV |
| Ellenville | EV |
| Napanoch | NO |
| Wawarsing | WG |
| Kerhonkson | KH |
| Accord | AX |
| Kyserike | KR |
| High Falls | HF |
| Cottekill | KO |
| Hurley | HU |
| Kingston | KN |

## SCRANTON BRANCH

|  |  |
| --- | --- |
| Cadosia | HD |
| Hancock | CO |
| Starlight | SR |
| Preston Park | ON |
| Lakewood | MC |
| Poyntelle | PN |
| Orson | BM |
| Pleasant Mtn. | SM |
| Forest City | CY |
| Carbondale Passenger | C |
| Mayfield Yard | SD |
| Jermyn | MY |
| Archbald | BD |
| Winton | WR |
| Peckville | KI |
| Olyphant | HO |
| Dickson | D |
| Throop | TR |
| Providence | DV |
| Park Place | PK |
| Diamond Crossing | DX |
| Scranton | JO |

## WALTON - DELHI BRANCH

|  |  |
| --- | --- |
| Walton | WN |
| Hamden | HM |
| Delancey | CD |
| Delhi | DI |

## NORTHERN DIVISION

|  |  |
| --- | --- |
| Sidney | SI |
| New Berlin Junction | NJ |
| Parker | GC |
| Guilford | GU |
| Summit | Z |
| Oxford | OF |
| Norwich | ND |
| Galena | NX |
| Smyrna | SA |
| Earlville | VI |
| Randallsville | RW |
| Eaton | AN |
| Morrisville | MA |
| Pratts | PR |
| Munns | MI |
| Valley Mills | V |
| Kenwood | CU |

## ROME BRANCH

|  |  |
| --- | --- |
| Clinton | CN |
| Clark Mills | CM |
| Westmorland | WD |
| Rome | R |

## UTICA DIVISION

|  |  |
| --- | --- |
| Randallsville | RW |
| Hamilton | HI |
| Pecksport | KS |
| Bouchville | BU |
| Solsville | S |
| Oriskany Falls | OR |
| Deansboro | DE |
| Franklin Springs | FN |
| Clinton | CN |
| New Hartford | HA |
| Canal Branch | RH |
| Utica | UA |

## NEW BERLIN BRANCH

|  |  |
| --- | --- |
| New Berlin Junction | J |
| Rockdale | RD |
| Mt. Upton | MU |
| South New Berlin | SW |
| New Berlin | NK |
| Edmeston | ED |

|  |  |
| --- | --- |
| Castle | X |
| Oneida | FD |
| Durhamville | DR |
| Fish Creek | FC |
| Sylvan Beach | FH |
| North Bay | BA |
| Jewell | VA |
| Cleveland | CD |
| Bernhards | BI |
| Constantia | CS |
| Central Square | CQ |
| Caughdenoy | J |
| Pennellville | VE |
| Fulton Broadway | JU |
| Fulton | FU |
| Arrowhead | AR |
| Oswego | OW |

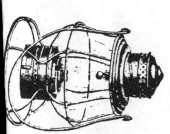

# CHAPTER THREE

THAT THE NEW GROUP of investors had high hopes for the Midland was evident in their choice of a corporate name. After the syndicate's representative, Conrad N. Jordan of the Third National Bank of New York City, had purchased the property for the sum of $4,600,000.00, the name they chose was "New York, Ontario & Western Railway Company." The only words retained were "New York"; the others selected were rich in connotation. "Ontario" signified a direct connection with the vast Canadian provinces, "Western" suggested an ultimate outlet at Buffalo and the West, "Railway" indicated the increasing number of English investors, in whose country "railroad" was looked upon as an Americanism. These earnest gentlemen could not foresee that car ferry service from Oswego to Canada would never amount to more than a trickle of traffic, that heavy investment and incredible luck would be needed to achieve a profitable enterprise through a western New York thickly infested with iron trails, that English capital was not the panacea for all the Midland's ills.

Nevertheless, after the purchase on November 14, 1879, and subsequent incorporation on January 21, 1880, Jordan was elected president and Theodore Houston secretary-treasurer. The list of directors in the *State Engineer's Report on Railroads* reveals a great deal more than a line-up of portly gentlemen encased in wing collars and surrounded with swirling cigar smoke. For example, it cataloged the eminent General Winslow and Horace Porter, friends and associates of George Pullman.

No secret was the fact that Pullman held a smouldering grudge against Vanderbilt and the New York Central for using Wagner sleeping cars on the "Water Level Route." Another figure less impressive in personal connections was Charles S. Hinchman of Philadelphia, representing the mysterious Buffalo, Chatauqua Lake & Pittsburgh Railroad. The only logical explanation for the merging of the Buffalo "paper" railroad with the O&W is that the time-worn dream of an eventual outlet on the shores of the Erie had not been abandoned. The notable Jacob Schiff, of Kuhn, Loeb and Company, who retained his personal and business interest in the line for many years, demonstrated by his presence the confidence of Wall Street that something could be made of the shaky corporation. All in all, the administrators looked like men of wisdom and substance, both of which were sorely needed by the reorganized line.

While the bondholders and holders of receivers' scrip were setting up the new company, municipalities and towns which had invested large sums in Midland stock were trying vainly to sell their holdings as a group to obtain funds to redeem the bankrupt railroad. Their efforts to keep some control in the hands of those whose money had built it went for naught when Oswego dumped her shares at a low price without consultation with the others. Financial loss was compounded with exclusion of any voice in company affairs.

Here began one of the most confusing periods in the entangled annals of railroad corporate history. The O&W reorganizers looked south from Middletown, saw two possible entries into New York (the Erie and the NJM routes), and wisely decided to build a new branch of their own, thereby avoiding the troublesome Erie and the poverty-stricken New Jersey Midland (later New York, Susquehanna & Western). Acquiring the charter of the Jersey City and Albany Railroad through its Midland Terminal Company, the Ontario then formed the North River Construction Company, headed by General E. L. Winslow, who concurrently served on the board of the O&W. Early

Robert F. Harding

Winter in the Midland country was seldom mild, especially at Walker's Cut on the Northern Division.

*No. 41* stands with her pilot wheels on the Weehawken turntable early in the 1880's.

*Larson Collection, courtesy Edward Baumgardner*

records indicate that preliminary construction work on the line began before the formation of the New York, West Shore & Buffalo (which utilized the surveys for the New York, West Shore and Chicago, which was never built) captained by another familiar figure, General Horace Porter. In January of 1881 the efforts of both the Ontario and West Shore corporations were pooled for the line below Middletown—the O&W connection on the Hudson to be made by a branch from Cornwall to Middletown. A lease dated May 12, 1881 gave the Ontario trackage rights to Cornwall. In effect, the O&W surrendered its North River charter to the new company. The reason publicly given for the pyramidal structure of interlocking companies was that in such fashion the O&W stockholders could share the profits of the West Shore enterprise. Some sort of profit-sharing took place, without a doubt, but there is no reason to believe that the ordinary investors got the lion's share. The most charitable comment would be that the financial arrangements were quite unusual.

Physical improvements on the line already built were of utmost importance because of the poor condition of the roadbed and the rolling stock. A citizen of Hamilton, New York, writing to the *Utica Herald*, complained bitterly of the service on the Utica branch. He said that the wheezy old engines were obliged to wait at each station to get up enough steam to reach the next. Trains were from 1 to 4 hours late, and the general public avoided traveling on the branch except in extreme necessity. Heavy chestnut and oak lumber was ordered for bridging as replacement for the shortlived hemlock characteristic of the early trestling. A roundhouse fire at Oneida destroyed the only storage and repair facilities, as well as the only turntable between Norwich and Oswego, in May. On October 12th, 1880, the bridge at Westfield Flats collapsed, throwing the local freight into the stream 15 feet below. No serious injuries resulted, but a property damage loss of ten thousand dollars was sustained.

*page 50*

The year 1882 saw the removal of both iron and telegraph lines from the DeRuyter branch for use on the main line. Strengthening of the Lyon Brook Bridge was begun with two new stone piers in the creekbed to support new iron posts. Although the severance of the Auburn branch seemed to the affected towns to be an act of deliberate malice, the administrators were exercising sound business judgment and by this and other economies were putting the O&W into the soundest physical condition it had ever seen.

The first issue of *Summer Homes* to be published by the O&W (the OM had published similar pamphlets in 1878 and 1879) was made available in June of 1880. This vacationer's guide to the resort areas of the Catskills was continued down to the last sad days of passenger service. The counties of Delaware, Sullivan and Ulster were rapidly changing from farm counties to resort areas, and the railroad could foresee a lucrative passenger business. Superintendent James E. Childs encouraged this economic revolution by dumping quantities of trout into O&W streams and outfitting passenger cars as "hunters' and fishers' specials." In later years, the company actually carried building supplies for prospective Catskill landlords at no charge. Just as the raw-boned rifleman had pushed out the redskins, only to be displaced by stolid farmers, so the dairymen found themselves jostled by the ever-increasing horde of city dwellers seeking the cool and quiet mountain slopes of the *Kaaterskill*.

Joint operation of the West Shore and the O&W began officially when time tables which treated both companies as one were issued in 1883. Early in January, the first O&W train from Middletown reached West Point and shortly thereafter the first freight of 10 cars of butter, cheese and hops from Oneida County followed the Hudson down to Weehawken with an estimated saving of 24 hours over the old route. Newspapers which had begun to doubt the miraculous quality of the Midland were climbing back onto the O&W bandwagon. In April the *New York Sun* stated:

> "If a stock like that of the Denver & Rio Grande road, which runs through a wilderness, and has never earned its running expenses (not to speak of its fixed charges) sells at $50.00 a share, there is no reason why the stock of a road running through one of the most prosperous sections of this State should sell as low as $29.00, especially when fully that amount has been paid in cash into the treasury by the original reconstructors, and no watering has taken place."

The wedding of the West Shore with the Ontario was followed by vigorous construction. The Oneida Castle Depot contract was let to Josiah Jenkins of Vernon for eight thousand dollars with the West Shore paying two-thirds and the O&W one-third, and a connecting spur at this junction (not more than a mile south of the O&W-NYC crossing) was projected. The two companies signed an agreement to occupy the Weehawken Terminal for ninety-nine years after August 1st 1883. In 1884, on the 2nd of January, the West Shore and O&W opened their Weehawken passenger station and began through service to Chicago. No worse time could have been chosen, for the ice, fog, dampness, and the necessity for a ferry trip from New York City made this service most unfavorable compared with the convenient New York Central facilities.

The inopportune inauguration of passenger service to Chicago may have been instigated by new financial troubles. Conrad Jordan and a group of coal dealers having claims against the Ontario made application for a receivership. Jordan's apparent concern for the company's economics was not shared by his fellow managers. They proceeded to elect John L. Nesbit as the new secretary-treasurer. Jordan found this no impediment to his career; he became Secretary of the Treasury under President Grover Cleveland. By February, North River Construction Company stock had fallen from 129¼ to 10, O&W stock from 42 to 10, West Shore stock from 36 to 8. The West Shore Company went into receivership on June 9th, with Horace Russell

*Robert F. Harding*

Summer brought central New Yorkers flocking to Sylvan Beach. Even off-duty trainmen headed for Oneida Lake breezes, including (at left) Chief of Police Wilson.

One of the first Ontario and Western passenger trains over the West Shore paused at the Haverstraw station long enough for a group picture of everybody in the area.

*Robert F. Harding*

The Mother Hubbard type, of which Number 1 is a fine specimen, became a conspicuous success on the O&W.

and Theodore Houston (Vice-President of the O&W) as managers. Heavy judgments were levied against the O&W for damages and unpaid bills in August. Oswego shop workers struck for three months' back pay in March. The 75 men involved resisted the company's deadline to resume work and only six were rehired when a full work force was employed again.

With a recklessness that seems unbelievable, the State Legislature in 1884 appointed Littlejohn, Low and Mr. Thomas to the Railroad Committee. This action drew newspaper fire and many public suggestions that these "railroaders" introduce bills to relieve entrapped and deceived railroad towns of their financial responsibilities. When corrective legislation was not on the horizon, retaliation by tax collectors was swift and frequent. In the town of Guilford a tax official boarded an express freight to seize the engine for taxes. So impressed and so confused was the local gentleman that when the crafty engineer began to move the train back and forth as though switching, the rural official lost his wits completely. He did not regain them until his dazed eyes recognized the Sidney yards. Frustrated and angry, he was forced to obtain other transportation home.

As though nothing of the kind were happening, workers were installing a side track and turntable at Fish Creek for the use of picnic trains. Numerous minor accidents—the collision of an express freight with the mail train near Trout Brook, the parting of an Ellenville passenger train within the Bloomingburg Tunnel, and the head-on collision near Pratts Hollow of an empty coal train with a light engine, all seemed to back up the advice of the veteran conductor who advised curious passengers: "I've been on the road fifteen years, and I've been turned over embankments, busted up in tunnels, dumped off bridges, telescoped in collisions, blown off the track by cyclones, run into open switches, and had other incidental divertissements of kindred nature, and I should say, gentlemen, the safest part of the car was that part which happened to be in the shop for repairs at the time of the accident."

By 1885, "unwarrantable and ill-advised assaults" had been made upon the company which necessitated a lengthy piece of prose composed by President Winslow for the *Fifth Annual Report*. The indisputable fact (not common knowledge at the time) that the North River Construction Company garnered $75,900,000 in railroad securities for its actual investment of $29,000,000 must have troubled those who did not share in the largesse. Riveted almost miraculously to the steep Hudson cliffs, swallowed at intervals by numerous tunnels and slashed in two by two drawbridges, the line above Cornwall was an impressive engineering achievement. Surrounded by fast-buck artists, undermined by watered securities and shaken by West Shore rate-cutting shenanigans, the corporate structure was no less an achievement. General Winslow cited the world-wide "depressed state of business" and "unexpected and serious obstacles, peculiar to the West Shore undertaking" for the disappointing O&W financial statement.

When the New York Central fastened its iron grip upon the bankrupt West Shore, consternation and fear for the Ontario was wide-spread. A new agreement between the Central and the O&W was soon effected, however, and resulted in a surprisingly satisfactory *modus vivendi*. The Middletown branch to Cornwall was turned over to the Ontario and trackage rights into Weehawken were assured. The fond dream of a vast railroad combine rivaling the great Eastern trunk lines had faded from the scene. For the second time in its history, the railroad missed its chance for greatness. Just as the Oswego Midland-New Jersey Midland combination failed when success was sighted, so the Ontario-West Shore combination came to a bad end. The parallel is even closer—President Winslow, like Littlejohn before him, bowed out of office just at the crisis.

The new head of the Ontario was a New York City railroad attorney who had been legal counsel for William H. Vanderbilt and for the Philadelphia and Reading Company. Thomas P. Fowler had as his first vice-president, John B. Kerr and as his second, Joseph Price of London, England. Before Fowler had completed his first month as head of the company, he was involved in a wreck fatal to two of his employees.

On the morning of February 13, 1886, *Train No. 6* was rolling south towards Liberty station under the competent hands of George St. John. In the sleeping car *West Point* were several O&W officials, including President Fowler and General Manager Childs. Within sight of the station, the train passed over a sand embankment undermined by water from a recent 36-hour rainstorm. The washout was a deceptive one, for a frozen crust of earth held up the tracks even though the sand below it had been scooped out by running water. When St. John's engine hit this stretch, the bank collapsed like an egg-shell under its weight. The locomotive plunged wildly off the track and toppled into the mud below. St. John and his fireman, Allan Lewis, were trapped in the engine cab and died there. In the dim half-light before dawn, Fowler had a solemn object lesson in railroad construction. Quicksand is not an adequate foundation for railroad traffic. The builders of the Midland had not bothered to draw in gravel or similar materials; the loose gritty earth from nearby cuts was more convenient. Three passengers were injured, but the unfortunate St. John achieved fame of a sort when he died. As the first O&W engineer to lose his life at his post, St. John was mourned by his fellow-employees—so much so that after a decent interval, Superintendent Childs ordered that no engines thereafter would be allowed to show the black draperies of grief. The solemnly-decorated steamers had made a great impression on the traveling public for one whole week, but the suggestions they made about the safety of O&W travel were not encouraging.

The "no mourning emblems" edict was not caused just by the Liberty wreck; it was a precaution against becoming known as the "Graveyard Route." In swift succession, Pat Fogarty, another engineer, and four trainmen were killed in line of duty. Fogarty was the victim of burns from steam and scalding water

Four men died at Fish's Eddy when one span of the Delaware River bridge was knocked down by a derailment.

from his standing engine; Conductors Howard Raymond and Ezra Smith and Brakemen Allen Embler and Emmet Johnson gave up their lives in a derailment at Fish's Eddy. The caboose of freight #40, along with six freight cars, was snapped off the end of the train by a rail broken beneath them. A bridge span was flattened and the cars took fire from the upset caboose stove. (Mrs. Smith was found pacing the floor in terrible fear, having had a premonition of disaster.)

Under Fowler's reign, many advances were made by the O&W. The Rome and Clinton and the Utica, Clinton and Binghamton roads were more carefully tied to the parent road by a D&H lease of June 1, 1886, which allowed O&W operation at a minimum rental of $75,000 per year. A new spur was built to the budding summer resort at Fish Creek, newly-christened Beacon Beach (later Sylvan Beach). Steamboats on Oneida Lake met trains here and afforded water excursions for O&W patrons. Picnic lunches among the shady groves and decorous bathing along the sandy beaches added to its attraction for vacationers. The Wharton Valley Railroad, running from the end of the New Berlin branch almost seven miles to Edmeston, was leased for 99 years in 1888. The last spike was driven at Edmeston in January of 1889, with rumors that Richfield Springs, 18 miles distant, would be the next important terminal on the Ontario and Western line. An extension of the Port Jervis and Monticello Company made a connection with the Ontario at Summitville, promising to produce new passenger revenues. One sour note was sounded when another periodic report on the "De-Ruyter Case" was published. The move to compel the O&W to re-lay and operate the Auburn branch was still alive in the courts after nearly ten years of abandonment. Of greater importance to the company than this legal annoyance from a dead branch was the new line into the Pennsylvania coal fields.

The Ontario, Carbondale and Scranton was a 54-mile railroad company which took shape from three short lines, the Hancock and Pennsylvania, the Forest City and State Line, and the Scranton and Forest City railroads. The Erie sought to prevent the branch from crossing its property at Hancock, but ultimately failed. Justice Forbes of the 6th Judicial District ordered the O&W to reimburse the Erie for its land and stipulated that the Erie must neither interfere nor compete by building a parallel branch. In expectation of heavy coal shipments, five hundred 20-ton coal cars were purchased and new motive power appeared. The most famous of these locomotives were the "Dickson hogs," with their wide Wootten fireboxes and cabs perched halfway down the boiler. These engines were so successful that "Mother Hubbard" locomotives outnumbered all other engine types as long as steam was king on the O&W.

When the Scranton branch was completed on June 30, 1890, British and Dutch investors could rejoice, for this was their pet project. More and more the control of O&W affairs had passed to interests outside the United States, and they soon showed business acumen that American speculators seemed to lack. Evidence that the Ontario was a late starter in the race to the coal regions was the obstinate refusal of Carbondale to permit a new railroad to operate through the city. O&W engineers, in true Midland tradition, backed off and made another approach which shot the tracks right over the amazed citizenry on a high trestle. Now the Ontario had justified its existence. From this date forward, the Ontario and Western would attain the dignity of an independent coal carrier.

Anticipating the rumble of heavy coal trains bound north out of Scranton, the main line came in for a complete overhaul. The Zig-Zag at Northfield made the trip between Sidney and Walton time-consuming and expensive. Accordingly, a contract was placed with Ward and Lavy of Newburg for the purpose of knocking a hole in Northfield Mountain, known locally as "Old Hardscrabble." December of 1890 saw the TNT explosion that permitted daylight to appear through the tunnel, and that almost asphyxiated two anxious engineers who stumbled forward in the haze to clasp hands through the opening.

Edmeston was the northern terminus of the Wharton Valley line of the O&W, now operated by the Unadilla Valley Railroad.

No. 74 pulled the first train through Northfield Tunnel, which replaced the old Zig-Zag in 1890. Superintendent Canfield is at left foreground.

*D. Diver Collection at Cornell, courtesy George C. Slawson*

The year 1886 brought to the O&W one of its most precious legends. President Fowler proudly took possession of the *Warwick,* a private car manufactured by Jackson and Sharpe. Old-timers maintain that this ornate official car was put at the disposal of President Grover Cleveland and that within the plush and mahogany privacy of this deluxe rolling mansion, he and his young bride, Frances Folsom, began their honeymoon trip. That there is little factual evidence for this story (even the celebrated historian and biographer of Cleveland, Allan Nevins, cannot confirm it) matters little. Its magnificent wood paneling, the gleaming brass beds, the elegant Victorian parlor with its cut glass chandelier, the spacious observation lounge and private kitchen made it the perfect conveyance for the newlyweds. And the *Warwick* was one example of the excellence of O&W equipment in the 1880's.

Not only were passenger cars "of new construction . . . [with] well upholstered Forney sittings" as a State Inspection of 1887 recorded, but trains 5 and 6 boasted Pullman buffet sleepers and reclining chair cars for the long trip from Weehawken to Chicago (via the RW&O and Wabash). Even the milk cars shared automatic couplers and air brakes with the more aristocratic coaches and parlor cars. And new freight cars were already in service on the Ontario Fast Freight Line between New York City and western cities on the Grand Trunk, Wabash and Rome, Watertown & Ogdensburg railroads.

Emerging from two major blows to its prestige—the failure of the Midland and the loss of its West Shore partner—the new Ontario company could leave its misfortunes behind and look ahead with confidence. Immigrants from Castle Garden streamed onto O&W coaches at Weehawken, making necessary two or more sections of through passenger trains. The milk trains were delivering a quarter million 40-quart cans from as far north as Edmeston on the rural Wharton Valley line. Passenger excursions averaged one extra train every three days. Almost 500,000 tons of coal were carried during the fiscal year

When delivered in 1886, the *Warwick* was the pride of railroad officials and a masterpiece of car construction.

Built by New York Locomotive Works in 1890, *No. 111* went on the scrap pile in 1935.

1890-1891. The new interchange with the New Haven system at Campbell Hall upon the completion of its Poughkeepsie bridge contributed to increased freight tonnage for New England. Prospects for the Ontario and Western were brighter in 1890 than at any time since the incorporation of the Midland. Surprisingly enough, the rejuvenated company might even fulfill the fondest dreams of the Midland.

CHAPTER FOUR

T HE ONTARIO COMPANY was finally making something of the
villainous old Midland. Appearing on the map like a prop for
the big sag in the main line at Hancock, the Scranton Division
was more than a prop; it became the firm foundation of an
important coal-carrier. Although gross income for the O&W
increased four-fold in ten years from ½ million dollars in 1880
to 2 million in 1890, the greatest revenue growth was ahead.
To assure itself of these coal revenues, the railroad company
advanced money to mining firms, taking mortgages at 6 per
cent interest.

The light iron, the pine and hemlock trestles, and the unbal-
lasted roadbed of the old Midland were too weak to hold up
under the pounding drivers of the new mogul (2-6-0) and consolidation engines (2-8-0) ordered in 1890-1891. Everywhere
along the route, a general "beefing up" was taking place. Coal
storage facilities, some of which were already available on the
Northern and Utica Divisions for fulfillment of previous coal
contracts with the D&H, were located at Weehawken and other
points. Trestles for transfer of anthracite to Hudson River
steamers at Cornwall and to Ontario lake boats at Oswego were
erected on these waterfronts. Until adequate facilities could
be found to cope with the great black flood, the O&W was
forced to reduce its coal traffic to manageable proportions. A
new symbol used by the railroad from this period onward was
contrived to signal the revival of the line and to help remove
the Midland stigma. Using the two letters "O" and "W," the
sign showed a gracefully curved "W" within the "O" circle.

*page 65*

# No. 1. NEW YORK, ONTARIO & WESTERN RAILWAY CO. No. 1.

## SCRANTON DIVISION.

### To take Effect at 12.01 A.M., Monday, July 21st, 1890.

| SECOND CLASS—NORTH BOUND | | FIRST CLASS—NORTH BOUND | | | | | | Car Room on Sidings. | Distance from Weehawken. | STATIONS. For the information and government of Employes only. | Distance between Stations. | Telegraph Calls. | FIRST CLASS—SOUTH BOUND | | | | | | SECOND CLASS—SOUTH BOUND | | |
|---|---|---|---|---|---|---|---|---|---|---|---|---|---|---|---|---|---|---|---|---|---|
| 233 | 235 | 211 | 209 | 207 | 205 | 203 | 201 | | | | | | 202 | 204 | 206 | 208 | 210 | 212 | 232 | 234 | 236 |
| Mixed | Way Freight | Pass. Local | Pass. Local | N.Y. Day Express | Pass. Local | Pass. Local | Pass. Local | | | | | | Pass. Local | Pass. Local | Pass. Local | Pass. Local | Ontario Day Express | Pass. Local | Mixed | Way Freight | Way Freight |
| | | | | 7.30 | | 1.35 | | | | NEW YORK ᴸᵛ | | H.D. | | | | | 7.35 | | 4.30 | | 5.15 |
| | | | | 7.10 | | 1.09 | | | | NEW YORK ᴬʳ / WEEHAWKEN | | C.O. | | | | | 8.10 | | 4.38 | | 5.25 |
| 2.45 | | | | 8.02 | | 12.35 | | | 161.13 | Hancock Junction | 2.07 | S.R. | 2.00 | | | | 2.00 | | 5.04 | | 5.52 |
| 2.38 | | | | 8.11 | | 12.21 | | | 162.20 | Starlight | 5.37 | O.N. | 2.05 | | | | 2.05 | | 5.17 | | 6.07 |
| 2.31 | | 1.56 | | 8.20 | | 12.09 | | | 167.57 | Preston Park | 2.96 | C.M. | 2.31 | | | | 2.31 | | 5.30 | | 6.20 |
| 1.45 | | | | 8.50 | | 11.56 | | | 170.53 | ...Comos... | 2.68 | P.N. | 2.37 | | | | 2.37 | | 5.45 | | 6.38 |
| 1.30 | | | | 8.57 | | 11.31 | | | 173.21 | Poyntelle | 3.17 | B.M. | 2.45 | | | | 2.45 | | 5.51 | | 6.42 |
| 1.20 | | | | 9.07 | | 11.21 | | | 176.38 | ...Belmont... | 2.05 | S.M. | 2.49 | | | | 2.49 | | 6.06 | | 6.58 |
| 12.55 | | | | 9.22 | | 11.09 | | | 178.43 | Pleasant Mt. | 2.55 | D.A. | 3.00 | | | | 3.00 | | 6.10 | | 7.03 |
| 12.47 | | | | 9.32 | | 10.57 | | 7.55 | 184.09 | Uniondale | 1.37 | C.Y. | 3.11 | | | | 3.11 | | 6.26 | | 7.27 |
| 11.30 | | | | 12.16 | | 10.48 | 7.40 | | 185.46 | Forest City | 5.98 | Y.D. | 3.30 | 8.18 | | | 3.30 | | 6.40 | | 7.45 |
| 11.10 | | 7.50 | 5.26 | 12.08 | | 9.20 | | | 191.04 | CARBONDALE YARD | 5.00 | C.A. | 3.36 | 8.30 | 10.05 | 2.05 | 3.36 | 5.40 | | 7.06 | |
| 10.57 | | | | 11.45 | 4.00 | 9.15 | 7.35 | | 196.04 | ...Carbondale... | 1.43 | R.A. | 10.10 | 8.35 | 10.09 | 2.10 | 3.30 | 5.45 | | 7.13 | |
| 10.52 | | 7.41 | 5.16 | 11.41 | | 9.11 | 7.31 | | 197.47 | White Bridge | 1.30 | | 14 | 8.39 | 10.14 | 2.14 | 3.34 | 5.49 | 7.28 | | |
| 10.49 | | 7.39 | 5.13 | 11.38 | | 9.07 | 7.28 | | 198.77 | MAYFIELD YARD | .90 | M.Y. | 7.02 | 8.42 | 10.17 | 2.17 | 3.37 | 5.52 | 7.30 | | |
| 10.43 | | 7.38 | 5.12 | 11.37 | | 9.07 | 7.27 | | 199.67 | ...Mayfield... | .50 | B.D. | 7.03 | 8.43 | 10.18 | 2.18 | 3.38 | 5.53 | 7.35 | | |
| 10.30 | | 7.33 | 5.07 | 11.32 | | 8.55 | 7.15 | | 200.17 | ...Jermyn... | 1.30 | H.O. | 7.08 | 8.48 | 10.23 | 2.23 | 3.43 | 5.58 | 7.47 | | |
| 10.13 | | 7.26 | 5.00 | 11.25 | | 8.55 | 7.15 | | 201.47 | ...Archbald... | 2.50 | | 7.15 | 8.55 | 10.30 | 2.30 | 3.50 | 6.05 | | | |
| 10.06 | | 7.21 | 4.56 | 11.21 | | 8.50 | 7.10 | | 203.97 | ...Winton... | 1.18 | D. | 7.17 | 8.57 | 10.32 | 2.32 | 3.52 | 6.07 | 7.53 | | |
| 9.58 | | 7.07 | 4.52 | 11.11 | | 8.46 | 7.06 | | 205.13 | ...Olyphant... | .76 | D.V. | 7.22 | 9.02 | 10.37 | 2.37 | 3.57 | 6.12 | 7.57 | | |
| | | 7.12 | 4.47 | 11.01 | | 8.41 | 7.01 | | 206.69 | ...Dickson... | .48 | | 7.26 | 9.08 | 10.43 | 2.43 | 3.43 | 6.18 | 8.05 | | |
| 9.52 | | 7.08 | 4.43 | 11.01 | | 8.37 | 6.57 | | 208.49 | ...Throop... | .97 | S.C. | 7.31 | 9.11 | 10.46 | 2.46 | 4.06 | 6.21 | 8.10 | | |
| 9.47 | | 7.07 | 4.42 | 10.61 | | 8.35 | 6.55 | | 209.67 | ...Providence... | 1.30 | | 7.33 | 9.13 | 10.48 | 2.48 | 4.08 | 6.23 | 8.13 | | |
| 9.41 | | 7.04 | 4.37 | 10.61 | | 8.33 | 6.52 | | 210.43 | ...Park Place... | | | 7.36 | 9.16 | 10.53 | 2.53 | 4.13 | 6.28 | 8.32 | | |
| 9.36 | | 6.59 | 4.34 | 12.58 | | 8.29 | 6.49 | | 211.91 | ...Providence... | | | 7.38 | 9.18 | 10.56 | 2.56 | 4.16 | 6.31 | | | |
| 9.30 | 9.30 | 6.55 | 4.30 | 12.55 | | 8.25 | 6.45 | | 214.18 | SCRANTON | 1.30 | | 7.41 | 9.25 | 11.00 | 3.00 | 4.20 | 6.35 | 8.40 | | 8.35 |
| 233 | 235 | 211 | 209 | 207 | 205 | 203 | 201 | | | | | | 202 | 204 | 206 | 208 | 210 | 212 | 232 | 234 | 236 |

All trains will run daily except Sunday.

Heavy figures (**12.01 A.M.**) denote passing points.

f Signifies that train will stop on signal for passengers or freight.

s That trains will stop.

1. Whenever any train is twelve hours behind time, it loses all rights to the track.

2. On single track all trains running SOUTH have an absolute right of track over trains of the same, or inferior class running in the opposite direction.

Trains moving towards Scranton will be considered south bound trains.

3. Trains will be run by Eastern Standard Time, which will be indicated by the standard clock in the Dispatcher's Office.

4. When but one time is given it is the leaving time, excepting that at passing points the time named for the superior train will be considered as its arriving time.

5. All trains will register at terminal stations.

6. All trains will come to a full stop before crossing any railroad at grade, and will not cross until the proper signal is given.

When the semaphore arm at the Diamond crossing of the D., L. & W. R. R. is in a vertical position by day, or shows a white light by night, the N. Y., O. & W. trains have the right to cross.

When a red ball by day, or a red light by night, is displayed from signal pole at crossing near Dixon Mill, the D., L. & W. R. R. trains have the right to cross.

C. W. LANPHER,
Supt. Transportation.

A. C. CARYL,
Assistant Supt.

J. E. CHILDS,
General Manager.

The construction of the new Pennsylvania branch was a matter of pride and prosperity.

Other traffic showed a less spectacular though steady increase. Free haulage of building materials for Catskill resort hotels and boarding houses was encouraging Ulster and Sullivan County building. Here, as in the anthracite business, "storage facilities" were inadequate to supply the need of the increasing numbers of New York City dwellers headed for country vacations. One of the most pretentious of these hostelries was that $60,000 edifice above Liberty, New York, whose construction the O&W management eyed with pleasure. Outings to Sylvan Beach, a park and bathing ground on Oneida Lake, achieved such great popularity that entrepreneurs from as far distant as Philadelphia came to look and invest their capital in cottages and hotels. Shuttle trains ran from the New York Central at Oneida, from the West Shore at Oneida Castle, from Utica and Rome by the round-about route through Randallsville. For many years men in gartered sleeves and bowler hats assisted their bustled and beribboned damsels up the steep steps of the O&W's wooden coaches.

The milk trains were running wide open from station to station, in a daily attempt to overcome time lost while grunting train crews loaded milk cans into the Middletown-shopped refrigerator cars. When the burden became so great that exhausted O&W workers complained and train schedules looked comical, an extra train was put on to Cornwall where both were combined. The company encouraged this increase by building creameries in likely rural settings and renting them reasonably to prospective shippers.

The O&W vine was flowering with new depots and milk plants. Vigorous life pulsed through the main stem as shiny and powerful new Mother Hubbard engines barked out of Scranton up the steep hill to Poyntelle, gathered momentum on the long downgrade and halted in the pungent atmosphere of overheated journal boxes at Cadosia, where the gritty cars were sorted and sent north and south to their ultimate destinations. The precipitous grades and awe-inspiring trestles

Inspection engine #26 here sports her second wooden body, having lost her first to fire at Liberty.

Inspection engine *#28* was converted from *No. 38* in 1889, scrapped in 1893, and the body transferred to old *#80*.

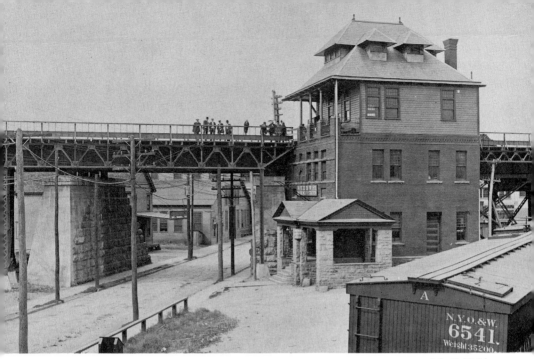

*John C. Walsh*

Three stories and a steam elevator were needed to get Scranton Division passengers on and off at Carbondale.

Ohio Falls built many of the narrow-vestibule wooden coaches like #65 which became O&W trademarks.

*H. L. Goldsmith*

The second Middletown station, shown here in an architect's sketch, was designed by a leading building designer, Bradford Gilbert, and contained a famous lunchroom (at far left).

Officials and excursionists were proud to be seen in the high and gleaming grandeur of the O&W's second inspection locomotive.

*William Capach*

An unknown post card photographer-artist resorted to a bit of trickery to place a Delaware River raft next to an Ontario and Western train near East Branch.

The second accident at the Fish's Eddy bridge tied up traffic for days in 1897.

*D. Diver Collection at Cornell*

which had been the bane of the Midland's existence became a positive asset from the passenger's point of view. The wild setting of the O&W reminded one of the exciting vistas of Western railroading.

Alongside the many picturesque waterfalls of the Stockbridge Valley, there occurred one of those spectacular accidents which by their destructiveness have an irresistible attraction. At the point where mail train *No. 2* had derailed about two weeks before, an exploding sheet of flame took three lives.

On March 13, 1893, Engineer Charles Hinchey whistled out of Oneida and opened the throttle of *No. 159,* a new Dickson Mother Hubbard engine, building speed to take his twelve-car oil train over the Eaton summit. At about 8:10 p.m., he stopped to take water at Munns (Munnsville) station, missing the water plug by about two car-lengths. Accordingly, he reversed, only to miss once more. His patience at an end, he spun the wheels and jerked his train into proper position. Unfortunately, this maneuver broke his train in the middle. Assuming that the crew would set the brakes sufficiently to hold the cars on the steep incline, he went about his tasks on the engine. But he had not counted on the attraction of the nearby saloon.

When the startled Hinchey heard the faint rumble of escaping oil cars, he blew his whistle for brakes. A subsequent investigation showed that most of the train crew was just not available at that moment. The night telegraph operator at Munns did testify that two lanterns came bobbing out of Ogden's saloon just after the crash, and it may be assumed that trainmen were attached to them. While the train crew was "laying the dust" with liquid refreshments, the scene was being set for the wreck. The violence of Hinchey's second stop had broken the last six cars and caboose loose from the train; these were held on the grade by setting the hand brakes. However, the head brakeman thought he could assist the engineer further by pulling the coupling pin between the first six cars and the balky locomotive. These cars could not be held and ran away from the surprised brakeman. With a thud they struck the standing cars, derailing some but sending the caboose and two oil cars rambling down the main line.

About two and a half miles north from all this activity a following freight train which also had oil cars next to its locomotive, *No. 166*, was digging into the Stockbridge grade. Mike Donahue of Oswego leaned out the right hand side, watching for a glimpse of the train preceding him. His companions in the cab were Martin Dalrymple, whose duties did not often allow him to look up from his coal-shoveling on the uphill climb, and LaFayette Burke, brakeman, whose seat was on the opposite side of the boiler, Mother Hubbard style. It is not unlikely that Burke was giving his fireman friend a hand with his work, for firing from the "kitchen" (the half-cab sheltering the fireman) on a heavy grade was man-killing labor. Assisting the train at the rear was engine 82, with W. Sweeney at the throttle. Whatever our conjectures about the occupations of the crew on *166*, it is certain that little or no warning was given before the marker lights of *Extra 159's* caboose came shooting towards them out of the blackness ahead. Donahue automatically set the brakes, threw the reverse lever, and whistled a warning just before he jumped. The shock of the collision sent oil gushing over the splintered caboose and cars, which ignited on contact with the live coals in the caboose stove and in the firebox of the engine. Within minutes, the splintered wreckage became a funeral pyre for three luckless men.

At a coroner's inquest, Michael Sheehan, trestle watchman near the station, testified that he saw at least two of *159's* crew go into the saloon. This substantiated the story of ghostly lanterns seen by Operator Wilber. After an early judgment that the testimony "seemed contradictory" the coroner's jury found, as did an investigating team of the N.Y. State Railroad Commissioners, that the accident was caused by employee failure. The damning phrase was "gross negligence." No one could quarrel with that decision, not even those accused.

Within the period from 1891 to 1893, the O&W had lost many good men in train wrecks. Engineer Albert Booth of Walton was the victim of a head-on collision between his freight train and a wild-cat (running without orders) engine near Guilford Center. Engineers Martin Sheedy and Fred Young, along with fireman Adelbert Cady, died in a high-speed crash of another wild-cat engine run by Sheedy and Cady. Sheedy had been called from his bed to take a relief locomotive from Norwich to Oneida for the morning milk train. The Night Express (No. 6) had taken the only available Oneida engine when its own broke down. Sheedy took the siding at North Norwich for No. 6 (which was running late) but forgot that the Utica freight was due. Near Smyrna, the two opposing trains met, to the shrill accompaniment of blowing whistles and screaming brakes. Less dramatic but equally serious wrecks made headlines at East Branch, North Bay, Mountaindale, Central Square, Wurtsboro, Hamilton and Oswego. During 1892, the railroad quietly placed stretchers on every train and in every station.

By 1893, the territory served by O&W milk trains extended as far north as Oneida, where Conductor J. E. Sharpe and Engineer Bill Harding steamed south promptly at 8:15 a.m., with engine #44 on the lead. No. 44 was the rebuilt veteran of the Liberty crash and Harding was another early convert from the RW&O. At each milk station the dissonant symphony of rattling milk cans was repeated until Norwich came in to view. Under a fresh crew, train No. 10 continued along the southern end until the dim lights of Weehawken terminal were reached at 10:30 that night. The milk business was not safe from "sharpers," for a few cans always arrived short. Careful measurement confirmed official suspicions and thus one local agent joined the ranks of the unemployed. He had been supplementing his salary by dipping just enough milk out of each can to make another full can of his own. A more amusing complaint of Weehawken employees was that ice used in milk cans was

*Robert F. Harding*

The railway boasted a marine division after coal transport became its major business. The *Ontario* was one of two tugboats maintained in New York harbor.

Official Car #25 was built by Pullman with open vestibules and arched windows. It went to the Detroit and Mackinac in 1917.

*John Stellwagen*

chopped too fine. By the time the cars arrived, there were few pieces large enough to be used in the family ice-box.

A magnificent passenger station was taking shape in Middletown, taking the place of the frame structure no longer adequate for the traffic. Constructed of Hudson River brick and Scranton sandstone with hard pine trim, the $50,000 depot advertised these on-line products along a 175-foot track frontage. Complemented by others along the line, notably at Sylvan Beach and Liberty, in the vacation country, this substantial symbol of Ontario health demonstrated the passenger appeal that the O&W scenery held.

Of course, the heirs to the Midland had acquired a number of non-paying passengers, too. As a part of right-of-way agreements, the original company had granted lifetime passes to these land owners. The Midland had been so open handed that many Sunday School picnic excursions traveled absolutely free of charge. And the free-pass policy had reached monstrous proportions when the old Midland crossed tribal lands of the Oneida Indians in the Stockbridge Valley. The O&W honored these earlier arrangements, undoubtedly to retain at least a modicum of good public relations.

The most colorful of these "deadheads," the railroad name for passengers riding on a pass, was making frequent short jaunts from Oneida to the Madison County seat at Morrisville. Nick Honyost was an Oneida Indian famed locally for his good nature and for his addiction to firewater. His trips, therefore, were usually of an official nature—the result of numerous convictions for public intoxication. Deposited at the county jail, Nick served out his thirty or sixty days with becoming cheerfulness and then rode the Maydole omnibus over Stage Hill to Morrisville Station. Somehow or other, he managed to acquire his favorite beverage before train time and climbed rather unsteadily into his favorite seat, the fireman's perch next to the locomotive boiler of the Mother Hubbard. The pleasant warmth of the adjacent boiler and the rocking motion of the engine

*D. Diver Collection at Cornell*

The first "home-made" Mother Hubbard rolled out of the Norwich shops in 1898, a Brooks single-cab engine with its face lifted.

One of the tough Dickson "hogs" perched on Carbondale trestle for this impressive photograph.

*D. Diver Collection at Cornell*

produced strange effects in Nick's system, and by the time he stumbled down from his seat, he was in very nearly the same condition which had caused his last jail sentence. Once in a while, poor Nick never reached downtown Oneida, but was on the judicial merry-go-round once more. Such was his reputation for honesty and good behavior, though, that he was later acquitted of a murder charge brought against him. The testimony revealed that Nick had cleaved the skull of an Onondaga brave who showed a disrespectful interest in Nick's wife.

The three-span bridge over the East Branch of the Delaware at Fish's Eddy collapsed under the weight of a coal train in 1897, just as it had done in 1886, when it claimed four lives. Less disastrous than the wreck eleven years previous, this most recent dunking attested to the fact that strengthening of the railroad line was still not sufficient for the traffic. In 1886, the end span had gone down, in 1897, the center span. Both accidents meant long delays in train movements, casualties to employees and bad publicity for the Ontario.

A nationwide business depression had seized upon the American nation in 1893, and heavy snows in the winter of 1894-95 had cut deep into the railroad's available funds for reconstruction and major repairs. By 1896, even the excursion business was in danger of being lost to a "trolley mania" that seemed about to make "railroad fever" look like a minor ailment. Additional worry was caused by the Ellenville line extension. It appeared that the Pennsylvania Coal Company would build a line parallel to the Erie, the PJM&NY, and the O&W Ellenville branch, into Kingston. The new state reformatory at Napanoch furnished added reason for the O&W to build north of Ellenville. By 1899, the coal company had changed hands and the O&W was able to plan its Ellenville and Kingston line.

At the end of the nineteenth century, the Ontario company possessed a rugged chunk of railroad, vastly improved over the Midland. The Pecksport Loop, a wholly-owned subsidiary line of 3.8 miles, bypassed Eaton, thereby reducing the grade between White's Corners and Randallsville from seventy feet to a more reasonable 26 feet to the mile. The Northfield tunnel cut more than 120 feet from the heavy grades from Walton at the south and Sidney at the north. The old switchbacks were gone, but the humor associated with them never died.

The story goes that Cal Sanford was having trouble coaxing engine 25 over the hill one night, and the presence of a company investigator made no impression upon either the locomotive or the crew. Long before the summit was reached, the laboring engine coughed and died. The man from Middletown spoke first in the awful silence. "Mr. Sanford, what is the trouble? We are not moving." Cal turned on his seat, smiled graciously and intoned, "My coal is poor and will not burn. My steam is gone not to return. And so we stopped upon the hill, the angels whispering, 'Peace, be still.'"

Besides the 1600-foot bore at Northfield, and the 3800-foot Bloomingburg tunnel, the O&W maintained two smaller tunnels on its line. Both the Fallsburg and Cadosia (Hawks Mountain) passageways were a little over 1,000 feet in length, and like the others were protected at each portal by semaphore or block signals. Northfield and Cadosia also displayed that primitive globe and pole device that gave "highball" its meaning. This tunnel collection, the countless timber trestles and steel bridges, the ten severe grades and the necessary pusher districts, all added up to a railroad line more like the Rocky Mountain-climbing Rio Grande than the level, unspectacular New York Central.

Savings on fuel consumption became more noticeable after these grade reductions on the main line, but another factor aided greatly. Small sizes of anthracite coal and culm (low-grade anthracite), available in abundance at the O&W's coal breakers, were being efficiently burned in the wide Wootten fire-boxes of the Mother Hubbard engines. For those uninitiated into the railroad fraternity, it should be pointed out that the engine cab was pushed out onto the boiler because of the

*Lillian Coe*

The new bridge over Lyon Brook was completed in 1894, strengthened to bear heavy coal trains.

Burt Wells piloted #99 around Oneida yard in the 90's. His full beard set him off from other crew members, who must have thought it a fire hazard.

*Robert F. Harding*

Arthur L. Hicks

Maydole's stage met all trains at Morrisville station, with Nick Honyost a steady customer.

Second #69 escaped the fate of her predecessor, which was auctioned off during the Midland bankruptcy.

Robert F. Harding

space requirements of these great yawning furnaces at the rear of locomotive boilers. The O&W was so pleased with its Dickson locomotives that they contracted with the Rome Machine Works to convert older motive power into the Mother Hubbard type. These powerful iron horses with the engineer's "cupboard" were finally outlawed because of the complete separation of the engineer from the fireman, but they became the O&W trademark and their numbers lasted as long as steam powered the railroad.

The ten-year period ending in 1900 was one of heavy expenses as well as of growing revenues, and improvement of railroad property took precedence over payment of dividends. Counting in the numerous loans to coal companies, the O&W had a surplus in 1890 of $345 and in 1900, of $1788. Control of the corporation rested with holders of preferred stock, who elected eight of the thirteen directors. In effect, President Fowler and the management held the reins. The protests against their policies of heavy capital outlay went unheeded. It was fortunate that this was so. Otherwise, the railroad might have reverted to rust and weeds and bankruptcy.

More and more, the O&W was sharing in the vital occurrences in American life. The Boxer Rebellion contributed troop trains and artillery specials, all bound for San Francisco and the struggle in China. The famed statesman, Elihu Root, specified that his special coach, the *Grasmere,* should take the scenic O&W route when he planned a western vacation. The Prohibition party chartered a special train on the Utica branch for a picnic at Madison Lake. Several hop-growers' picnics jammed the wooden coaches with farm workers whose agricultural efforts were in direct opposition to the appeals of the Prohibition party. These producers of beer's flavoring journeyed to Sylvan Beach for their revels; the more staid teetotalers preferred the sober atmosphere of the countryside. Minstrel troupes, opera companies, and circuses with intriguing and forgotten names like "Sells-Floto," "Walter L. Main," "Irving's

Imperial Midgets," "Gus Hill's Minstrels" rode gaudily-painted cars to their small-town destinations. Governor Teddy Roosevelt found it convenient to route many of his official trips via the Ontario. All in all, the New York, Ontario & Western Railway was achieving a prominent position in the transportation of goods and people.

With a string of varnish behind, *No. 4* pounds through Mayfield Yard, passing the loaded coal cars that spelled O&W prosperity

CHAPTER FIVE

I N 1902, a new feeder line
opened for the company. The
Ellenville and Kingston Railroad was built and financed by
Ontario and Western, which had acquired the charter of the
Kingston and Rondout Valley Railroad Company. Rolling easily
northeast through the old Dutch and Indian settlements of
Napanoch, Kerhonkson and Cottekill, the E&K followed the
abandoned pathway of the pioneer Delaware & Hudson Canal.
Almost at once, the anticipated increase in passenger traffic
materialized, for dispatchers' diaries began recording a recur-
ring phrase—"Convicts and keepers for Napanoch." The State
of New York was pleased to have such convenient transportation to its new reformatory on Rondout Creek.

The 28-mile E&K extension bridged the gap which existed
between the Erie at Port Jervis and the New York Central
(West Shore) at Kingston. The Port Jervis to Monticello Company had reconsidered its earlier decision to ignore the Midland on account of its bypassing Monticello, and in 1889 built
a connecting link with the O&W from Huguenot. A direct and
unusually straight (for the O&W) line now ran between Port
Jervis on the Delaware and Kingston on the Hudson, bisecting
the parent company's main line at Summitville. Although these
two subsidiary railroads were treated as separate and distinct
companies on the O&W books, in effect they were operated as
one branch and later became known as the Monticello, Port
Jervis and Kingston Division.

*Harold M. Whiting*

Runaway coal trains were constant threats to life and limb of the Scranton trainman. This pile-up near Starlight took four lives one night in 1901.

The long rural haul of the railroad's milk trains meant that ice-houses be kept well supplied, and shivering workers at Fargo labored all winter to fill the need.

*Glenn Buell*

Almost from the start of train service into Kingston, one of the O&W's pioneer enginemen, Eugene Bearss, established himself as the idol of children along the route. Promoted to the right-hand side in 1874, Bearss earned the nickname of "Bootjack" by wearing leather boots and carrying his indispensable bootjack strapped to his traveling case. When Bootjack squeezed his bulk through the cab doorway on *No. 3*, the Mothe Hubbard's accommodations were amply filled. So great was his attachment to the railroad that he retired to a shanty the company provided near the wye at Summitville, passing his last days among the sights and sounds and the friends he loved best.

Not all O&W men were as fortunate as Bootjack Bearss. The demands made upon men and machines were heaviest on the booming Scranton Division. Just two days after Christmas of 1901, the wreck of a runaway coal train cast a pall of gloom over the town of Carbondale and threw four families into mourning. Part of the story of the wild, destructive ride came from Eugene Fitzgerald, an 18-year-old boy from Sidney, who had hidden himself on the tender for a free ride home.

Train #229, consisting of engine #201 and forty-four loaded coal cars, left Mayfield yard at 10:30 p.m. for Cadosia. When the creeping train reached the crest of the hill at Poyntelle, it was 6 a.m. The 22-mile trip had consumed almost eight grueling hours. At this summit, the two pusher engines cut off and Engineer Melvin Whiting was left to control the heavy train with just eighteen cars equipped with air brakes. The remaining gondolas could be retarded by muscle power applied to the hand brakes by three brakemen and Conductor Grant Smith.

From the moment that he made his first brake application, Whiting undoubtedly sensed the danger which threatened his life and the lives of his crew. The rails were slippery with a coating of ice and the wheels refused to adhere to them. Before Preston Park appeared out of the winter morning gloom, Whiting had whistled for brakes and the men scrambled over the ice-encrusted coal, tightening brake wheels as they went. The train's speed slackened for one hopeful instant and then the cars surged forward on the slick iron. His efforts to check the runaway found useless, the engineer continued sending out chilling shrieks on the whistle, more like cries for help than signals. The brakemen slid and stumbled so badly on the jolting cars that their efforts came too late. Young Fitzgerald, clinging to the side of the wild steel creature, realized that disaster lay ahead, but, like the other passengers on this mad ride, he knew that jumping meant sure death. The roar and rush of the speeding train filled their hearts with terror.

In the middle of a sharp curve just below Starlight, a flange on *201's* pilot truck broke and the plummeting train sailed off the rails into the semi-darkness. The locomotive plowed into the ground at an estimated eighty miles an hour and crunched to a stop. Carried by the tremendous momentum, the following cars skidded into the overturned engine, dumping ton upon ton of coal around the fallen iron horse. Conductor Smith and Brakeman Walsh were still fighting their way along the cars, wrestling brake wheels with a strength born of fear. When the crash came, they leaped clear of the rolling cars and saved themselves. Fitzgerald was miraculously spared by a lurch of the locomotive which threw him away from the pile-up.

Superintendent R. B. Williams of the Scranton Division had the sad duty of recovering four buried bodies from the carnage. Besides Whiting, the dead were Charles Millard, his fireman, and two brakemen, Pat Duffy and Richard Budd. The town with the romantic name of Starlight, Pennsylvania was the unlikely scene of one of the most depressing accidents on the Scranton Division.

The wreck was a symptom of the growing problem of coal choking the single-track out of the Lackawanna valley. With Scranton Coal and the Elk Hill Company committed to send all tonnage over O&W rails under loan agreements, with new spurs opening to Capouse and the Raymond washery, the congestion was getting out of hand. In 1902, company officials (who were later to see eight miles of loaded D&H coal cars at Mayfield waiting for clearance, crews and engines) decided to double-track the most crowded section, Cornwall to Cadosia. And even though the line now averaged one iron or steel bridge every two miles, there were still 21 of wood and 71 unfilled timber trestles. To help equalize the largely seasonal demand for anthracite, the O&W also heaped large piles of small coal sizes at Middletown during the summer months.

Such conditions continued to take their toll of men and machines. Mike Hoey gave his life in the second of two accidents within a year. The first one occurred on July 21, 1901. Engineer Hoey of freight *No. 34* sat in *No. 184,* holding the main line at Parker for the appearance of *No. 23* from the south. When *23* puffed into view and continued working steam past the switch, Hoey left his engine, which settled the argument alone with the pugnacious *No. 187.* The collision amounted to little more than a firm nudge, but it brought the offending engineer, Lew Eaton, a temporary suspension. His only excuse was that he fell asleep at the throttle. He had come on duty just fourteen hours before.

The second accident involved no one but the unfortunate Michael Hoey. Running on West Shore trackage from Weehawken, he had pulled up at Valley Cottage for water and discovered an overheated driving box on his side. (*No. 175* was a Mother Hubbard, with the drivers beneath rather than ahead of the engine cab.) Resolving to keep his eye on the trouble spot, Hoey whistled off and began the twenty-mile run to Cornwall. Separated from him by the boiler, brakeman Tom Gorman and fireman Charlie Jackson noticed the unaccountably high speed approaching Cornwall, and tried to warn the engineer by yelling through the speaking tube. Now past the station and a red block signal, Conductor Knox and his caboose crew proceeded to set brakes. Gorman climbed around the front of the locomotive to investigate but found the right-hand seat empty.

The Port Jervis line put train crews and passengers close to nature, and the O&W encouraged this pleasant impression with rustic depots like this structure at Hartwood.

The two piers at Weehawken were built expressly for transshipment of the black flood that thundered out of the O&W coal fields.

Forced to climb through the window when he was unable to shove the front door open, the worried brakeman saw the engineer crumpled on the deck. Hoey was dead.

The exact cause of death remained a mystery, although it was obviously due to a heavy blow to the head. Who or what had struck him down? The only clue was the engineer's missing cap. A careful search revealed the cap lying near the end post of a bridge near Fort Montgomery. In his last inspection of the running gear, Hoey had apparently leaned out the cab window, forgetting the close clearance of the approaching bridge. Mike Hoey's brother, Bartholomew, kept the family name on the engineer's roster until his fatal heart attack on his engine in 1935.

The Ontario company, in order to alleviate the clogged condition of single-track weighed down by heavy and frequent strings of coal cars, was spiking down second-track as fast as crews could work without delaying trains. Stockholders looked upon the construction with mixed emotions. The additional trackage assured better earnings in the future; for the present the project precluded any dividends on the common stock. Ever since 1885, the 3000 Ontario share-owners had protested vigorously against the corporate arrangement by which preferred shares elected a majority of company directors. Impatiently they watched treasury surpluses devoted to seemingly endless improvements to the railroad property. What was apparent to the most cantankerous investor was the able leadership guiding the fortunes of the New York, Ontario and Western Railway.

The rank and file of railroad workers was growing along with the increase of traffic. As more "old heads" were assigned to the summer passenger runs into Orange, Sullivan and Delaware counties, fresh crews appeared on the gritty decks of O&W locomotives and on the swaying cars grinding out of the coal fields. The longer strings of cars kept extra crews jumping and pusher engines hot.

Night and day, the Oneida pusher nudged freights up the Stockbridge grade and then dropped back into the yard to await another southbound train. From 1902 to 1904, a slight young man appeared, shovel in hand, at the gangway of this shuttling locomotive. Before he went to his work on his nightly chores, Fireman DeForest (Pat) Diver could be seen carrying pails of water up to the second floor of the Victorian brick building which accommodated passengers at Oneida. There he set up one of his first darkrooms. Photography fascinated Diver early in his life, and he never lost his interest in picture taking. Nor did his affection for the O&W ever falter. The present generation is indebted to him for the superb picture collection which mirrors the life of the railroad.

The use of passenger car running gear, air brakes and refrigeration (the O&W claimed to be the first railroad to run refrigerated milk cars) on milk equipment enabled the company, among all such carriers into New York City, to capture first place in total cans shipped by 1902. Three regular milk trains required extra sections almost every day. And the second section of *No. 11* (northbound) figured in a spectacular head-on collision with its opposite number, *No. 12* (southbound) on August 3rd. To add to the coincidence, *No. 11* had engine *No. 144*, *No. 12* had *No. 143*. Both locomotives were year-old Mother Hubbards, the former from Cooke, the latter from Dickson.

Ben St. John, son of the first O&W engineer who died at his post, was rattling along at 20 miles per hour towards a meet with *No. 12* at Chiloway. Andy O'Neal, a trusted engineman promoted in 1881, was approaching the Chiloway switch from the north at 40 miles per hour. The hazardous separation of engineer and fireman of these cab-in-center engines played its fatal role once more in this accident. O'Neal, on *143*, never slackened speed near the switch and Conductor Ducolon in the combination coach behind found reason to regret his decision to leave Walton without his air brakes connected. Late

MAP OF
New York, Ontario
& Western Ry.
1907

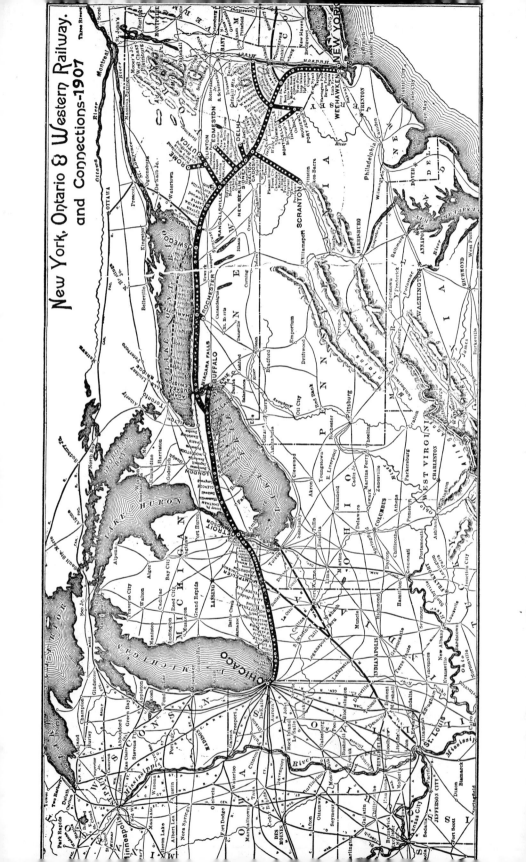

New York, Ontario & Western Railway
and Connections-1907

already, the crew had not welcomed the additional box cars added there because a severe storm had upset the schedule of the regular freight. One of these unwanted box cars had no air brakes and the crew did not wait to have an air pipe installed under the one lacking such equipment. Therefore, Ducolon's brake valve was useless; control of the train brakes (on the first five cars) was left solely to the engineman.

One-half mile south of the meeting point, St. John stared with disbelief at the sight of a speeding train, under full steam, rapidly closing the short distance between them. In an instant he had shut off steam, yanked the air brake handle, opened the sand pipe and leaped out the window. The impact of the collision rammed the tenders hard against the engine boilers, punctured the smoke boxes so that one slid neatly into the other, and tumbled both hissing monsters onto their sides in the adjacent field. In the deafening uproar of crunching metal and gushing steam, four men died: Engineer O'Neal and his fireman, Bob Reese, of the southbound train and M. J. Tully and E. Sweet on the northbound. St. John's timely leap carried him straight through a barbed wire fence. He lost only a pair of pants and his dignity.

As important as milk was becoming to the economic life of the O&W, this traffic was almost inconsequential compared with the coal tonnage rumbling over the line. It was inevitable that larger railroads with no direct line into the coal fields should show a new interest in the Ontario. In 1904 the New York, New Haven and Hartford purchased controlling interest with the acquisition of 291,600 shares of common stock. Their subsidiary, the Central New England, provided the connecting link with the O&W at Campbell Hall, via the Poughkeepsie Bridge. Although no changes in O&W management resulted, the New Haven was primarily interested in the lucrative coal business. Unofficially, at least, the old Midland changed from a convenient corridor for upstate products and became a busy coal carrier. The emphasis on bulk freight shipments of

There was little left to rebuild when Train *No. 3's* locomotive exploded near Luzon. She went to the scrap heap and three men to glory.

Another unsolved mystery was the wreck of *143* and *144* near Hortons in 1902. Engineman Andy O'Neal died with the secret — why did he pass the switch at Chiloway against orders?

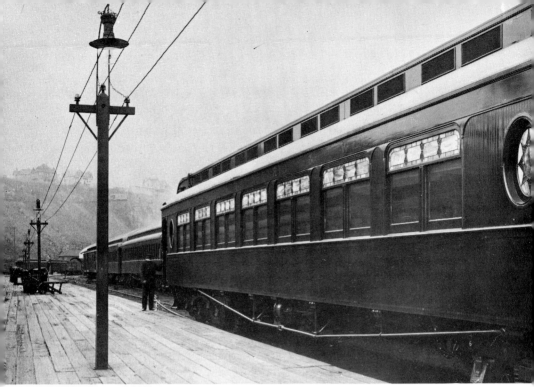

*John Stellwagen*

Parlor car *#88*, the *Hudson*, posed here at Weehawken, was a distinguished addition to the elegant passenger equipment of the Ontario & Western. Its gleaming wooden sides, stained-glass windows and accommodating porter made railroad travel an experience to remember.

Coasting into Bouckville Station on the Utica Division, Second *No. 13* passes the Genessee Fruit Company building, an important shipper until the trucks took over much of the agricultural business.

*Lillian Coe*

coal moderated the early efforts to build passenger traffic and encourage local industry.

If the demand for coal kept the rails shining in the winter months, the resort-seekers produced the same result during the summer. More than one and a half million passengers were carried in 1903 and the prospects were bright for a sizable increase each year thereafter. Luxurious parlor cars with their wide vestibules contrasted strikingly with the older coaches which retained their narrow entrances. These "vestibule chair cars" were the company's substitutes for the Pullmans run on neighboring lines. In every respect they equalled or exceeded the standards set by America's pace-setters in traveling elegance. Returning to the Midland practice of naming equipment, the O&W chose those romantic names of rivers and streams suggestive of the wild natural beauty of its scenery. The gilded *Oneida* took its place beside its gleaming sisters, the *Beaverkill* and the *Mamakating*. Even if O&W passenger schedules were "flexible," the customers could arrive late in comfort.

Happy endings are seldom current in real life, but an episode at Fallsburgh approached the miraculous. As *No. 1* drew up to the station one hot summer morning in 1901, the platform audience watched a young woman, almost hysterical with grief, helped down the coach steps by sympathetic volunteers. The story told was heart-rending.

She had set her baby on a trunk next to an open coach window so that he could watch the passing countryside. As the train emerged from the tunnel just south of the Fallsburgh depot, the coach gave a sudden lurch, throwing the child headlong through the window. The mission of retrieving a dead baby from the right-of-way was accepted reluctantly by Bill Brock, night operator at the station. Just before reaching the north portal, he discovered a child, grimy and very much alive, playing happily in a pile of coal screenings which had been dumped next to the tracks. The tearful mother was only too glad to embrace her youngster, dirt and all.

*page 98*

To save time and expense for passenger trains on the Monticello line, a cut-off was constructed from Roses Point to Valley Junction in 1904. This allowed removal of several miles of parallel trackage through Port Clinton and North Huguenot, and saved a half hour's travel time. It also allowed the O&W to better compete with the Erie's more direct route to Port Jervis, with transfer to the O&W for the short trip to Monticello.

The directors' decision to pay a dividend on common stock in September of 1904 answered the long-standing objections of shareowners to the policy of improving property out of earnings. The declaration also ended the controversial voting trust which had kept control of the company in the hands of the preferred stockholders (*i.e.*, the management). Each common share drew a $3.00 dividend in January 1905 and payments continued, with few exceptions, until 1928. Preferred stockholders received dividends for the same years, and for 1900-1904 and 1930-1935 as well. In effect, the 1905 dividend allowed the New Haven to place its own men on the Ontario Board of Directors.

The report for 1907 by Carl Snyder, titled *American Railways as Investments* paid tribute to the abilities of the O&W management but cautioned that the road itself was "enormously overcapitalized" with an investment per mile "about the same as that of the New York Central, with gross earnings per mile nearly double that of the Ontario."

And strive as they might, O&W officials could never match the on-time records of the New York Central. Making up time on passenger runs required skill and daring on the part of the O&W enginemen. The constant twisting and turning, the incessant climbing and descending demanded firm hands on the throttle, judicious use of the brake valve. On February 13, 1907, Train *No. 3* was sacrificed to this attempt to get back "on the card."

Engineer Will Gadwood of Walton, was pushing *No. 70* as hard as he could, for he was running late. Sharing the single cab was J. D. Valquette, a fellow engine runner, and Fireman Martin Mullen. Although no one could reveal the cause of the explosion, the circumstantial evidence is that enginemen often ran with boiler water dangerously low, creating greater steam pressure but making cold water injection very hazardous. Whether this hypothesis is correct or not, the indisputable fact is that *No. 70* shattered herself into thousands of flying metal fragments, hurtling her three occupants into the air and throwing the train down the 20-foot embankment just south of Luzon. The engine was a total loss, and so, unfortunately, were the men who rode her. Gadwood lived but a few hours and died without uttering any word to explain the disaster. Although the passengers were badly shaken up, none of them was seriously injured.

Such serious incidents, plus other minor train collisions and derailments during the early 1900's, were the background for General Superintendent Canfield's official order that speed limits would be observed. He set 40 miles per hour as the maximum safe speed on descending grades and curves, and 50 miles per hour at all points. A great many runners violated this rule, thereby avoiding reprimands for late time caused by obeying it. No sane bystander stood close to a piece of level, straight O&W trackage when a scheduled train was due. The suction was often enough to carry him a half-mile free.

One passenger man whose speed did not always seem consistent with O&W geography was Bill Young. His railroading fame rests on one memorable trip over the Northern Division. The Chicago Limited, which ran from Weehawken to Oswego and then followed the Ontario shore via RW&O to the Wabash, was regularly several hours late towards the end of the O&W run. An engineer of Young's temperament must have seen this as a personal affront. With the help of a substitute dispatcher at Norwich, he made a valiant effort to overcome *No. 5's* unsavory reputation.

As usual, the through train approached Norwich yard in the evening darkness, the glowing headlight an advertisement of its tardiness. When Young climbed into his seat and whistled out of the station, no one suspected the wild ride that was to come. Now the Northern Division as far as Oneida had kinks and turns, grade crossings and bridges which required an engineman to be cautious in controlling his train. Besides these rather rigid requirements, *No. 5* had five scheduled stops to make between division points. Young knew one fact which led him to overlook a few rules.

The regular DS was off duty that night and Superintendent W. C. Hartigan safely at home. The dispatcher's assistant, Walter Osgood, was left with responsibility for the entire division. Traffic being exceptionally light that evening, no one had reason to expect anything exceptional to happen. But *No. 5* was already rocking along the main line at great speed.

As Conductor Jim Carroll picked up his clearance card at Randallsville, Osgood was surprised at the arrival time reported. At Oneida, surprise turned into astonishment. Had they known, the bobbing passengers could have taken some comfort in the knowledge that their engine driver had run for Lieutenant-Governor on the Prohibition ticket. If the conductor so informed them and ruled out intoxication, there was always the suspicion that the man had gone mad. Jolting into curves and surging ahead on the straightaways, Young made every ounce of steam count. Under his expert hands, the Chicago Limited ate up the 100 miles in exactly 110 minutes. His average speed was an unheard-of 55 miles per hour.

For two days following, the office of Superintendent Hartigan was in almost continual use by those employees involved in the record run. The Northern Division super was firm but fair; disciplinary action was taken only against the engineer, who earned a vacation without pay.

Gradually the Scranton branch was being double-tracked to match the Cornwall to Cadosia section, giving the O&W some relief from head-on collisions, jammed coal sidings and short tempers. The Capouse spur line was lengthened to connect with

*Blanche Sanford*

Oneida Castle Station was a "split-level" serving the high-speed Utica to Syracuse trolley line above and O&W steam trains below. For years this was the starting point for local Sylvan Beach trains.

Coal trestles had a strange attraction for O&W trains and this jumble at Port Jervis was one of the two unique accidents in which no one was badly injured. The other occurred at Hamilton when startled crewmen joined the "Flying Diesel Corps."

*William Capach*

*Jack Farrell*

The "Teakettles" saw long and honorable service in passenger work. Here one of the handsome ten-wheelers pauses for a drink late in her career.

On one of her first runs, "Bullmoose" *No. 351* passes *No. 1* of the Delaware and Northern at East Branch, with a dynamometer car in tow.

*Karl E. Schlachter*

the Lehigh Valley Railroad at Sibley, Pennsylvania, adding one more traffic interchange.

Improvements and additions to the locomotive roster were made almost every year, but the years 1910 and 1911 witnessed the return of the single-cab locomotive to a position of prominence on the O&W. The W class was made up of 26 sturdy Cooke consolidations which were promptly christened "Long Johns" by the shopmen and operating employees. Such was the impression a clean boiler line made on those accustomed to a shanty lodged midway down the engine. They took their place in the roundhouse next to the P class, nicknamed "Orries" (probably because they came to the assistance of the O&W at the turn of the century just as the "U.S.S. Oregon" steamed in to control Santiago harbor in the Spanish-American War).

The favorites of the O&W stable, however, were those four Brooks ten-wheelers which were delivered in 1911. Numbered from 225 to 228, these graceful engines *looked* fast and they were. Purchased to pull main-line passenger trains, they soon earned a reputation for ease of handling and high speed. The E class soon came to be known as "Teakettles," but their performance showed that their fragile appearance was deceptive. They went like the wind. The more experienced Mother Hubbards they labored beside were tagged "Shanghais" by some imaginative wit who noticed the resemblance of the high cabs to Chinese pagodas.

The same year brought major changes in the line-up of officials. Curtis Knickerbocker, a native of Morrisville who walked into an engineering department position from graduation at Princeton, retired January First, of 1912. He had supervised an almost complete rebuilding of the Ontario line, including the reconstruction of the famed Lyon Brook bridge. The resignation of President Fowler and the deaths of General Manager Childs and Superintendent Canfield followed soon after. And 1910 was the last year that Billy Harding (promoted in 1871) would hold the throttle. Failing eyesight caused his retirement, leaving his son Jesse to carry on the family tradition at the right-hand side, and another son, Bob, who became one of the most faithful O&W fans. His O&W collection, at the date of this writing, is undoubtedly the largest of its kind in the country.

In 1912, another engineman came to the end of the line. Fred Kingman had survived a collision with the second section of the Chicago Limited at Parker, a small station below Norwich. Two years before his accidental death, as he was dropping back to Sidney with the pusher, Kingman failed to observe the approach of the immigrant-laden passenger train until much too late. He landed in a bruised heap in the Limited's tender, but three passengers died in the splintered wreckage of the first coach. At Galena, Kingman's luck ran out.

On March 12, 1912, Engineer Kingman was peering ahead of train 89, a regular northbound freight, his view obscured by drifting snowflakes. One mile north of Galena (North Norwich) station Extra 104, John Adams, engineer, appeared like a spectre out of the whiteness of the landscape. Kingman jumped to his death. His fireman, David Ivory, escaped this fate, but Fireman Irving Cole of train 104 was killed. The crew of Cole's train had misunderstood an order to take the siding at Wilbers.

Not all O&W accidents ended in tragedy, however. Some were close to slap-stick comedy. For instance, in October, 1913, a restless Mother Hubbard rambled untended down the DL&W line from Norwich until it reached Oxford. A confounded Lackawanna engineer blinked unbelievingly at the nonchalant approach of a totally unfamiliar locomotive, running straight into the face of passenger train 811. No serious injuries resulted, but Superintendent Hartigan had some embarrassing questions to ask. Who fired up 191, leaving the throttle open? And why were the switches all lined up for the DL&W tracks?

The most comical of all Ontario wrecks was due partially to the weather, partially to other factors. Sunday, March 1, 1914 saw so much snow that trains on the road stalled and

Middletown in 1913 was a busy passenger terminal, with long strings of coaches waiting for their locomotives to coal up at the trestle in the left foreground.

When President Fowler resigned at the end of 1911, this employee delegation, all pressed and shined, rode #26 and Car 25 to his Warwick home for formal presentation of the loving cup in the foreground. From the left: 1) Peter Johnson, section foreman; 2) John Wilson, baggageman; 3) Ed McNiff, engineer; 4) Herbert Kennedy, hostler; 5) T. Frank Cullman, freight agent; 6) William Pohlman, shop foreman; 7) Levi Hasbrouck, porter; 8) Edward Henry, conductor; 9) Jackson Mattison, trainman; 10) Mortimer McGraw, trainman.

engine fires were dumped as water reached a dangerously low level. The Northern Division plugged tight at Morrisville and Cleveland, and the Southern Division fared worse. Heavy-powered snowplows and helper engines running light in their wake were the only train movements until Tuesday, when the line above Livingston Manor became unblocked.

That same day, an impressive caravan steamed down from Summitville to clear the Port Jervis branch. Conductor Jim Morgan's line-up was Engines *140* and *177*, a snowplow known as a flanger, caboose *8154* and Engine *13* in reverse. The combination of ice at the Ball Street trolley crossover, excessive speed, and the proximity of the Coonrod coal siding led to a startling series of events. Opinions differ about why the train pounded up the steep incline to the coal shed, but the fact is that it ran through the switch, steamed up the siding, banged open the coal shed doors, pushed out the south end of the shed and toppled awkwardly off the trestle to the frozen ground 20 feet below. Crew members sailed out of windows and doors in all directions, landing in the coal piles and bales of hay under the trestle enclosure. Fortunately, when the commotion ceased, the flanger hung halfway between the end of the track and the pileup below, causing only minor injuries to the thirty laborers inside. *No. 13* and the caboose stopped just short of disaster inside the ravaged walls of the wooden building. Not one of the men assigned to the run had ever traveled the branch before, and no pilot had been provided.

The existence of the O&W as a relatively independent line was well established by this time. The New Haven's control extended to the election in 1912 of its president, Charles S. Mellen, to the top O&W post, but he resigned in a year. John B. Kerr, originally a West Shore civil engineer, was elevated from vice-president in his place. Another threat to the free-lance standing of the Ontario was the unsuccessful deal by which the New York Central tried to trade the Rutland to the New Haven in exchange for the Ontario & Western. The New

York Public Service Commission disapproved, viewing with alarm any repetition of the West Shore story. Competition with the New York Central was a valuable function of the smaller railroad.

Actually, the O&W threat to Central prosperity was slight. The Ontario attracted very little through traffic over its torturous route. Its main-line passenger trains 1 and 2 (the *Ontario Express*) and 5 and 6 (the *Night Line,* or *Chicago Limited*) were patronized mainly by upstate travelers or by immigrants assigned to the O&W on a quota basis. Even the sensible route change of 1912 which shunted 5 and 6 by way of Earlville and the Chenango branch of the West Shore impressed few travelers. Connection at Oswego was a farce during bad winter weather; in reality, Oneida was the northernmost terminus of the O&W when the blizzards roared off Lake Ontario.

If the dainty little ten-wheelers were the beauties of the motive power department, 1915 saw the advent of the beasts. Twelve lumbering behemoths squatted on ten small driving wheels, and propelled themselves painstakingly over the rails. Powerful but slow, the X class soon became the "Bullmooses" to the enginemen, with an ironic reference to the spectacular failure of Teddy Roosevelt's third party. Patterned after New York Central engines, the Bullmooses gained an early reputation as back breakers. Engineers and firemen found themselves slaves to the mighty thirst and hunger of the Bullmoose. The X class spent countless hours under the water spout, at the coaling trestle and significantly, standing at the shops. After experimental use on the main line south of Cadosia (after delivery at Sidney, their massive proportions and unsteady motion under steam necessitated their crawling slowly through Northfield tunnel at the end of a string of freight cars), they were demoted to helper service on the Scranton Division. Beginning in 1940, they started off to the boneyard, long before their more ancient compatriots. Impressive and slow, dramatic and awkward, loud and inefficient, these locomotives symbolized the road they served.

Coal was the life-blood of the railway, but agricultural products helped by filling its boxcars. Besides the profitable milk runs, the local freights were earning their way during the summer months. On one July day in 1917, the consist of *No. 38* included 1600 bags and 225 baskets of peas, 1700 crates of lettuce, 22 crates of eggs, 5 tubs of butter, and 1 crate of chickens —supplying enough freight for six loaded cars. And almost every hamlet along the Northern Division was represented. To encourage these rural pursuits, the O&W and Cornell University sent out a farm and dairy demonstration car to exhibit at small-town sidings.

Summer breezes ushered in the traditional shuttle trains between Castle Station and Sylvan Beach. The shuttered Sylvan Beach depot shook out its winter dust and the unused rails of the loop which carried vacationers down to the waterfront assumed their seasonal glitter. On July 4, 1917, almost 6,000 excursionists landed at the long open pavilion that served as the passenger waiting room. The big union station (first built to serve West Shore at one level and O&W at the other) at Oneida Castle was the transfer point for third-rail trolley passengers from Utica and Syracuse to the wooden coaches below. High seniority employees transferred from freight jobs to handle the seasonal rush. Conductor Jim Carroll regularly left main-line passenger runs for the crowded, more lively Beach trains. Old-timers will recall other names—Al Nash, Ed Belisle, Gene Smith, Gus Rowe and many others. The year 1917 would be one of the last years that the old green frame building would serve happy vacationers. Within a few years, Castle Station would be a vacant monument to progress.

Mixed trains, however, were part and parcel of the railroad's service to upstate communities. Carrying everything from a few cans of milk in the way car to the local minister in the combination coach, these leisurely travelers ambling down rural rights-of-way were homely reminders of dependable, friendly service. No branch-line train was more unique than the Rome

Fred Kingman's first serious accident gave us this view of the splintered interior of an immigrant coach which slid onto the locomotive he struck head-on.

local. Each week day the crew made two round trips with its miscellaneous cargo from Rome Station to Clinton (whose wedge-shaped depot still retained "D. & H. C. Co." from the 1880's when the Canal company operated both the R&C and the UC&B). Keeping clear of trains 59 and 60, which ventured onto the main line as far as Norwich, was the most important of their operating responsibilities. This "express" covered the 13-mile branch in forty-five minutes, but the "peddler" consumed one hour, with luck.

The uniqueness of the Rome local was not in its daily performance; this was typical of every railroad branch in the United States. The unusual character of the train was its crew. From the one-eyed conductor to an ancient and unlettered (he was discharged from RW&O for inability to read and write) brakeman, the trainmen were all memorable characters. They were:

> Ward Silliman, engineer
> George Doorhammer, fireman
> William McLaughlin, conductor
> John Welch, brakeman
> Michael Claffy, brakeman

Their various infirmities gained them the unofficial title "The Cripple Crew," but the term was an affectionate one for men who were admired and respected by all who knew them. E. B. Stanley of the Clinton Knitting Company was one of these. He jotted down a few lines of verse which should be judged not as literature, but as a simple tribute to these branch-line railroaders:

> Let me tell you the story of Billy Mack,
> Who runs the local to Rome and back,
> On a one-horse train, on a one-line track,
> With an old crippled driver with a hump on his back,
> And a one-eyed baggageman cooped in the hack,
> And a two-fingered brakeman by the name of Jack,
> And sometimes it gets there, and sometimes it gets back.

The train makes two trips, over and back.
You don't know when it leaves or if it will ever get back.
The old bus may bust or she'll jump the track
Or the bumpers may buckle and break up the hack.
When the train starts out, Mack takes his stand
On the back of the hack with a wave of his hand,
And you'd think it was time to start up the band,
And the train was the greatest in all the land.
Bill gathers the tickets in a manner quite grand
And greets all the passengers on every hand.

But one day, there was an ice storm and alas and alack,
When the train came thundering down the track,
The flag that was flying, we notice was black
And the local came back without poor old Jack.
Still the old Rome local goes over and back
With its worn old engine and old line hack
And Billy stands out on the hack's back stand
And bids you farewell, with a wave of his hand.

Among O&W workers in this era an *esprit de corps* existed
that extended into high places. Conductor Percy Spring, who
came from the New Berlin local to main-line trains 5 and 6,
could always get a chuckle from his standing joke about the
shop foreman at Norwich. W. W. Daley had a voice like thunder and a ready laugh. Whenever a locomotive's exhaust indicated that the valves were set incorrectly, Spring would imitate
the irregular sound by chanting: "Daley fixed me—I ain't
t'blame, Daley fixed me—I ain't t'blame." And President Kerr
had time to visit with an old friend at Hamilton, plugging
the main line with his special train.

Such was the resurrected old Midland at the beginning of
World War I. The burden on United States railroads caused by
heavy wartime traffic became difficult to manage and coor-
dinate, until the country's rail transportation facilities were
seized by the government. The O&W was no exception, and at
noon of December 28, 1917, Director McAdoo assumed control of the company. On June 12, 1918, Joseph H. Nuelle,
the road's General Superintendent and Chief Engineer was
appointed Federal Manager.

Waiting for the shuttle from the Beach to Oneida was a part of summer vacationing for thousands of upstate New Yorkers in the Good Old Days.

Joining the happy throngs who rode to the shores of Oneida Lake were these proud trainmen who found a welcome change of pace on the Beach runs during the summer.

The hill out of Mayfield wore down both men and machines as the long heavy coal trains ground slowly and interminably out of the anthracite fields. For the work, the Bullmooses were well fitted.

# CHAPTER SIX

THE WAR YEARS were busy years, but except for the troop trains and heavier freight hauls, the O&W operated much as it had in the past. Soldiers patrolled the line, guarding against sabotage of any of the railroad's weak points, its bridges and tunnels. No attempts were made upon these objectives, but there was excitement and destruction just the same.

On the evening of August 12, 1918, *Extra 307* southbound was just breasting the hill between Apex and Cadosia with a loaded troop train behind. Engineer Kinch, Fireman Joy and Brakeman Baker were suddenly enveloped in scalding steam which exploded from the firebox into the engine cab. Guy Kinch, drenched in searing water and steam, made his way over the tender to reach the emergency brake valve in the first coach. Finding the door locked, he collapsed on the platform within sight of puzzled boys in khaki. Fortunately, Conductor Paddy Kerins noticed that the passing siding they were to take for a northbound extra had gone by with no slackening of speed. The brake application flattened every wheel on the train, but a worse disaster was avoided. The crew found three seriously injured men, one of them, Baker, so badly burned that he died in Carbondale hospital.

Such tragedies were unusual, although the railroad management complained of a lack of adequate roadbed and equipment maintenance under the United States Railroad Administration. During one short period of time, thirty broken rails were spotted by overworked section gangs between Roscoe and Livingston Manor. USRA Director McAdoo had a short-term goal —the winning of a war—and that objective took precedence over all complaints. However, the O&W was looking ahead to many years of peace, and preferably, of profit. Though the patriotism of the railroad management should not be questioned, they saw the meager repair policy of the USRA as "short-sighted," to put it mildly.

When the government released the O&W to its owners once again, the company made claim for government compensation in excess of the amount allowed under the Transportation Act of 1920. After long and arduous negotiation, a compromise figure of $500,000 was accepted a year later.

One of the rehabilitation jobs which this money would help pay for was a rebuilding of the Middletown Station Restaurant. A destructive fire in 1919 had left Southern Division travelers without convenient meal facilities along the route. Long after other railroads had adopted buffet and dining cars, the Ontario & Western clung to its ten- or fifteen-minute "meal stops." When the New York-Chicago trains were a bright hope in the company's imagination, Pullman Buffet cars had been tried, but the Pullman contract was soon superseded by the use of company equipment for the relatively short passenger runs. The practice of halting trains to allow passengers to race for the lunchroom must have caused countless cases of dyspepsia. But there were compensations. When the squeal of train brakes announced the arrival of another avalanche of famished humanity, the long rectangular wooden counter was already set precisely and neatly to accommodate the panting customers. The pastry baking of the Seeholzer brothers made the rush worth while, and their delicious doughnuts brought about better public relations than did any more elaborate advertising. When Car 30 went out on an official trip, the pantry was stocked from the restaurant supplies. Right down to the last days of its operation, when Superintendent Fred Hawk reluctantly closed the famed Wickham Avenue lunchroom, the reputation of its crullers spread. It is fortunate that the Oneida Station served few passengers and closed down early, for it had been notorious for its foul coffee.

Summer passenger travel into the Catskill foothills was fast approaching bonanza proportions. In 1920 almost two million vacationers stepped off the green wooden coaches into the refreshing atmosphere of wooded mountain slopes. Hotels and boarding houses were bursting at the seams with O&W's human cargo. At this point, the company found itself in a curious position. A post-war lag in freight business and the unsatisfied claim against the Federal government left the treasury very low. To relieve "much discomfort and inconvenience from crowded trains," the managers were reduced to buying second-hand coaches. Four fifteen-year-old passenger cars came rolling in from the Detroit and Mackinac, and two additional parlor cars, christened the *Ulster* and the *Orange,* were acquired from the St. Louis Southwestern shortly thereafter. Finally, in 1922, twenty new steel coaches were ordered from the Osgood Bradley Company. Even with these to supplement summer passenger equipment, the demands for added capacity did not abate. Revenue from this source continued to climb.

Repairs and replacements to the rolling stock were given top priority during the '20s because of a shop strike which made heavy repair and reconditioning work almost impossible. When the Labor Board ordered a wage reduction for the shopmen, they walked out and strike-breakers walked in. These new men required guarding and company housing to discourage violence, and more important, they were not able to turn out engines and cars as efficiently as their predecessors had. To add to the railroad's woes, the coal strikes of 1919 and 1922 reduced coal revenues drastically. Then, at the resumption of mining, coal shipments were so heavy that the run-down motive power simply couldn't handle it. By November of 1922 every industrial siding, passing track and shop track was filled with loaded cars. Until the road was finally unblocked, the situation was enough

The hazy atmosphere of the Norwich roundhouse was convincing proof of activity on the railroad at this Northern Division point.

In the days when the depot was the center of town activity and the arrival of the morning train an exciting event, this scene was set at Fish's Eddy, New York.

The docks at Cornwall were peaceful enough on Sunday, with the O&W tug tied up and long ranks of coal cars awaiting Monday's trip onto the trestle.


**The** important junction at Cadosia and the long bridge over Cadosia Creek deserved an official photograph during reconstruction to handle increasing coal traffic.

to drive everyone from super to conductor to distraction. And to further complicate the revenue picture, the Interstate Commerce Commission then reduced freight rates by 10%. . . .

Because of the feebleness of its steam power and in spite of uncertain earnings, the Directors approved the purchase of four powerful Mountain-type engines from the American Locomotive Company. Having proved themselves on steep mountain grades of western railroads, they were thought to be rugged enough for the stiff Ontario and Western requirements. These handsome iron horses were numbered from *401* to *404* and assigned to light freight and heavy passenger runs. The Y class, as they were designated, buckled down to their work with such ease and economy in their first year of operation that six identical engines were delivered the next year. Lacking the tractive effort of the homely X class, the "Light 400's" made up for this shortcoming with speed, ease of handling and beauty of line. To this day, Engineer John Fagan will say affectionately, "Every mile was a smile on the good old *401*." Their weight and size, like that of the Bullmoose, was such that they were unsuitable for the Northfield Tunnel and the lighter, curved Northern Division roadbed.

The roadbed in all districts was in poor condition to support any engine class after the cloudburst of Sunday, June 11, 1922. On that day, washouts kept wrecking crews and emergency track gangs jumping. For more than a week, traffic was interrupted at one or more points. Train *No. 509* was undermined as it stood at South New Berlin, three feet of brown water stood in the Oneida Station, three separate washouts between Oneida and White's Corners demanded the attention of Chief Engineer Nuelle and Maintenance of Way Engineer Heidenthal, and the two pile drivers and clam-shell digger rushed from trestle work at this site to other catastrophes on the Port Jervis and Scranton Divisions. Milk trains 9 and *10* began running to Utica and then by way of the New York Central to Oneida, avoiding the Munnsville section. A few other trains were detoured over the

"Water Level Route," introducing Ontario operating employees to the "high iron." The well-ballasted, heavy rails of the Central had none of the sharp curves of the Northern Division, and they were actually higher rails—the O&W's twisting right-of-way had early convinced its engineers that a low rail would be less likely to break under sideward stress. Less web made rails stronger and safer.

Safety was becoming a real worry for the Ontario and Western. Grade crossing accidents were no longer isolated incidents involving hay wagons, errant cattle, drunken pedestrians and the like—strange new names for mechanical conveyances appeared in accident reports. As the motoring public took to New York State highways, a few unfortunates came into calamitous contact with O&W trains, mangling their Wintons, Stars, Flints, Chandlers, Appersons, Marmons, Whippets, Overlands, Hupmobiles, and in large numbers, their sturdy black Fords. While the automobiles seldom won in a direct contest with the iron horse, its opposition was keenly felt in another way. The freedom from timetables, water stops, trainmen's moods and the other restricting factors gave the auto a tremendous advantage over travel by rail. Because of dwindling passenger traffic, the railroad's schedule was reviewed and changed to account for the changing pattern of human traffic. During 1925, the first twelve-month period in which sizable mainline passenger losses occurred, the Company itself experimented with the internal combustion engine.

Ugly despite its shining coat of maroon paint, Motor Car *No. 801* was one answer to the problem. This Sykes rail bus measured forty-two feet over couplers and boasted a Sterling 150 horsepower gasoline power plant. Like its highway counterparts, it had a gearshift, rugged enough to operate so that enginemen dreaded a call for a run on the *801*. On its first assignment, the iron snout headed out of Summitville for the off-season trip to Monticello. When vacation time arrived and a steam train replaced it, the motor car lumbered north to substitute for trains *41* and *42* on the Norwich-Oswego run.

Although the car was less than a whopping success on the long hill into Monticello, the management was so impressed with its operating economies (it required a crew of only three men—engineer, conductor and baggageman) that three Brill cars of similar construction were ordered. These were of the gasoline-electric type, with greater passenger-carrying capacity, more powerful engines, improved heating systems and smoking compartments. *No. 804,* one of the two largest (seventy-five feet over couplers), was bought especially for the *Delhi Flyer,* the branch-line train which connected the county seats of Utica and Delhi, both located at two feeder-line extremities of the Ontario and Western. On July 15, 1927, the *Flyer,* with Hans Hansen at the controls, struck a truckload of peapickers north of Solsville, killing two and injuring sixteen others. The gas buggies still constituted a hazard to the railroad and to themselves.

Although grade crossing eliminations had been under way as early as the turn of the century, these auto-train tangles spurred both the railroad and the Public Service Commission to greater efforts. Several such projects were in the construction stage in 1926, the most ambitious of which would do away with sixteen crossings at grade in the city of Fulton. The State furnished the funds for the work, a half of which was loaned to the railroad, to be repaid over a long term.

Other improvements during this period were the enlargement of Northfield Tunnel (site of the old Zig-Zag) and purchase of waterfront property at Oswego. These two moves were made in anticipation of freight increases from Oswego harbor. For years the Federal government marked time on planned upgrading of the water facilities there, and the work was not completed until 1933. The general decline of business in 1933 nullified any real benefit to the railroad. The tunnel work at Northfield Mountain helped somewhat in increasing revenue, for now larger modern boxcars could be routed through the

*page 122*

This peaceful scene along the right-of-way of the Utica Division charmed passengers but also is typical of vast stretches of country trackage devoid of freight-producing industry.

bore. But the "great port city of Oswego" remained a third-rater no matter what the boosters could do.

Traffic of all kinds began a steep downward plunge after 1925. For instance, one ominous directive cut off the summer trains between Castle and Sylvan Beach in mid-August, long before Labor Day. The reason given was "light business and wishing to use motor car in other service." The throngs of bathers and picnickers of past seasons who once patronized the railroad had shrunk to the point where one of the "Toonerville Trolleys," as the rail cars were called, was running almost empty to and from the central New York playground.

At the northern end particularly, travelers were avoiding the O&W in such numbers that the regular Norwich to Oswego trains were discontinued in 1929. In 1930, the joint agreement between the Company and the West Shore at Castle Station was cancelled and the agency closed. The Depression days made themselves felt in the closing of many way stations, the assignment of caretakers to others and the consolidation of several. The raging fire which destroyed railroad buildings at Valley Mills in 1926 went undiscovered far too long simply because the caretaker was not on duty. When finally discovered, the flames had made such headway that the freight house, coal sheds, ice house and milk station were burned to the ground. The way freight engine sent from Norwich dragged out two milk cars only slightly scorched, but the Valley Mills depot was eliminated even more efficiently than the hard-pressed railroad might have wished.

The abrupt change in O&W fortunes was still viewed as temporary, for it paralleled the experience of almost every other business enterprise in the United States in the 1930's. Layoffs were unquestionably serious matters to the employees, but there were less serious occasions. Some enginemen seemed completely unequipped to cope with the intricacies of the gas buggies and treated them with a minimum of respect. Passengers praised their cleanliness, speed and smooth ride (although

*page 124*

the short seat backs were uncomfortable on long trips), but the men who nursed them over the rails had a different opinion. Had old Nels Waterman been alive, there would be a few dents in their sheet metal, for he expressed his annoyance with a number of well-placed kicks to the boiler head.

Engineer R. E. Rowe was of a similar turn of mind. A most pleasant fellow off duty, Rowe assumed a tight-lipped silence when his run began. In the hours on duty he remained grimly uncommunicative until he stepped off his engine. When he was assigned to *804*, his face seemed to grow darker, and on one most memorable occasion he finally expressed himself, fully and forcibly. When the motor conked out at Randallsville, he collected his tools and dived into the engine compartment. An agonizing period of tinkering and testing brought a murderous scowl to the face of the sweating engineman. At last he erupted from the doorway, flung his wrenches far out into the adjacent field and addressed a few well-chosen (and unprintable) words to the motor car and to the company which had been so addle-headed as to buy her in the first place. There were, as the public learned to its dismay, rather strong opinions on the subject. For a relatively short few years, however, the four gas cars served their purpose very well.

By 1930 traffic conditions rather than operating difficulties dictated a transfer of *Nos. 802* and *804* to the parent road and the New Haven also inherited the *803* in 1935. Before this transfer, the last regular passenger assignments for the little tin wagons were on the Kingston line. The ugly duckling of the group, aging old *801*, retired to the rust and weeds of a Middletown siding in 1939. There she remained for many years until she was dismantled and her ancient body used as a shanty.

Even though the improved automobiles were claiming more and more passengers, devotees of the rumble-seat and the side curtain, two segments of this traffic remained almost intact. Winding, crowded and hilly roadways north from New York into the Shawangunks and Catskills discouraged motorists by

*#308* cuts out a string of freight cars to the tune of a sharp exhaust at Cadosia against a wintry backdrop.

For the benefit of the photographer, the crew of W class *324* stoked up the fire and pulled away from the double-header freight at Randallsville.

the thousands and contributed greatly to the O&W treasury. A much smaller group of upstate college boys entertained one another by making fun of the indispensable service of the railroad they called the "Off and Walk." The little passenger depot at Hamilton saw the arrival and departure of vacation specials, football specials, commencement specials and of the infamous *Cannonball*. The *Cannonball* rolled into Hamilton from the south in the dead of night with a miscellaneous cargo of assorted freight and weary college boys. It stopped everywhere, or to put it more accurately, it stopped nowhere often. The old mixed train became a local legend.

Most of the old-timers from the Midland days had also passed into legend and history. In 1930 Conductor Bill Oliver could still tell tales of the first passenger service over the West Shore in the '80s when he envisioned a vast railroad empire emerging from the West Shore-Ontario combination. Good-natured Heamon Purdy was a fading memory, for he left the Midland early in his career for the New York Central and died in 1906. Another "old-head," Grant Wilson, had been on the retired list since 1926, with forty-six years of faithful service behind him. Wilson braked and fired in the risky days of link and pin, lost an arm while coupling cars and advanced to become the company's Chief of Police.

Effective January 1, 1930, President John B. Kerr resigned, ending a long and successful railroad career that began in the engineering department of the West Shore. His successor was Joseph H. Nuelle, another professional engineer with twenty-three years of experience with the Ontario and Western. The new head of the Company faced a multitude of problems which neither faster freight schedules nor the heavier new Mountain-type locomotives could completely overcome.

Again in 1929, the need for better motive power was extreme. Twelve elderly engines, including some of the original Dickson hogs and Rome steamers, were due for retirement. In their place, ten large modern freight haulers were purchased through the issuance of Equipment Trust Certificates in the amount of $660,000. That the company had no trouble financing such new equipment may be taken as a clue to the confidence placed in Ontario management and Ontario assets.

By 1932, coal freight earned $5,844,900.00 for the year, slightly more than in 1926, one of the peak years. On the other hand, more than offsetting this increase was the drop in passenger revenue. This item plummeted from over 2½ million dollars to a little over a half million during the same years. From the mid-twenties on, the *Annual Reports* echoed the phrase, "Passenger business continued to decline . . ." Trains *41-42* on the Oswego to Norwich run were eliminated in 1929, the last Port Jervis train ran in 1930, Monticello became a bus stop from Fallsburgh Station. The following season reduced the physical size of the timetable by one-third, with cutbacks everywhere. The stately old Oneida Castle Depot was abandoned, and but one daily passenger train made the mainline round trip above Sidney. For all intents and purposes, year-round travel on the O&W was severely limited to a few Southern Division strings of varnish—the *Mountain Limited*, the *Roscoe Express*, the *Twilight*, the *Delaware Valley Express*, the *Ontario Express* and the *Saturday* and *Sunday Specials*.

Operating economies were effected in every department, from the top to the bottom. The New York City accounting force moved to the Middletown Station and administrative offices in Gotham found less expensive quarters there than Grand Central Terminal. Ticket windows at a number of small communities were shut down and passenger facilities transferred to freight houses. In an effort to slash fuel consumption, the Pecksport Loop, which avoided the precipitous Eaton grade, was finally designated as mainline for all trains. The old county seat at Morrisville saw only the daily milk trains and local freights, the second blow to its pride since the removal of the county offices more than twenty years before. If the seriousness of the railroad's financial situation had escaped the notice of

Two steamers enjoy a moment of rest at Middletown. Oldtimer *244,* vintage of 1904, and newcomer *409* stand back to back in the sunlight.

A useless antique, the O&W's first motor passenger car was consigned to rust and oblivion at Middletown after a decade of passenger service.

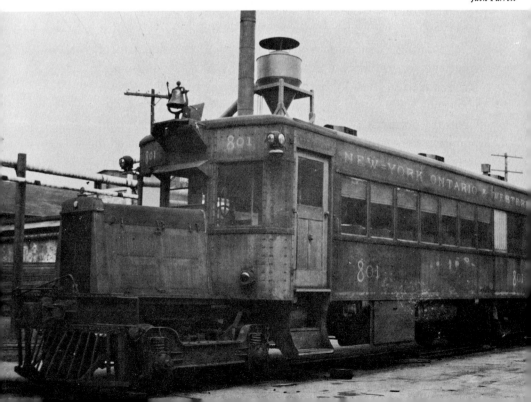

*Jack Farrell*

Even in the wintertime communities on the Southern Division depended on O&W passenger trains. Fallsburg furnished a handful of impatient travelers.

Once the temporary end of tracks for the Auburn Branch, this station at Merrifield (Scipio Center) became a general store and town clerk's office.

*Robert F. Harding*

some employees previous to 1932, then an announcement in February of that year made the point most forcefully. The wages of officials and workers alike were cut 10%.

Although income seemed to be rising, from a deficit of $250,000.00 in 1930 to a net income of $778,000.00 in 1932, the worst days were ahead. Anthracite coal shipments continued as the railroad's specialty, accounting for about 70% of total tonnage in the early 1930's. One significant fact was that the number of locomotives in service dropped from 177 in 1930 to 145 in 1932, with no additions to the roster.

Any improvements to the property of the railroad were those mandated by absolute necessity, or in the case of crossing eliminations, those ordered by the Public Service Commission. These latter projects, which amounted in some cases to major reconstruction, placed a great burden upon the harassed Company. In the words of President Nuelle, "The policy of the State of New York for the elimination of grade crossings is progressing so rapidly that it is working a hardship on your Company." Ironically, the highways which were reducing O&W passenger fares were also forcing the Company to expend larger sums to make these roads safer and more efficient.

Examining itself thoroughly to find any possible sources of income which might have been overlooked, the Company dug into its records and came up with a piece of property that it had not used for over fifty years. The abandoned Auburn Branch was still on the books. In late 1930, Claims Agent Marsden and Assistant Engineer Fagley took to the dirt roads and began parceling out the overgrown right-of-way to neighboring farmers. Passing the summit at Crumb Hill in their rubber-tired sedan, they must have recalled the tales of train crews stranded in tons of drifted snow, shoveling the white stuff into the engine tank for water or jacking up the drivers so that the water pumps could be kept in motion. Certainly they knew of the pitched battles fought between the tax collectors and the Midland men, when depots burned and cars were seized and reclaimed, stolen and re-stolen in a frenzy of righteousness by both sides. The old cause was forgotten and the sale of railroad land was soon accomplished.

A deficit of $78,000.00 in 1934 grew to be almost $331,000.00 in 1936. The business slump of that year, in conjunction with a cut in government expenditures and labor conflict in the coal and steel industries, made it impossible for the railroad to pay the interest on its Refunding Mortgage Bonds due in 1992. Other factors which made this decision mandatory were the mild winter weather, which reduced coal demand and a scaling down of freight rates by the Interstate Commerce Commission in 1933. Under the law, the Company had six months in which to make good its financial obligations to bondholders.

Three important coal producers in the Lackawanna Valley were closely allied with the Ontario & Western through the railway's ownership of stocks and bonds of the Scranton Coal Company and the Penn Anthracite Collieries. The first of these went into trusteeship and ceased operation completely in May of 1937. Penn Anthracite defaulted on the bond interest in July of the same year. A third coal company, the Monarch Anthracite Mining Company, struggled along, operating from its Pine Brook breaker at Scranton. The crux of the Ontario and Western problem, as was pointed out in ICC reports on the bankruptcy, was the failure of its affiliated coal mines. The flow of Pennsylvania's black diamonds was the life-blood of the New York, Ontario & Western. Mine floods and costly strikes had very nearly pinched off the supply for all time. That King Coal would ever be unseated by petroleum seemed remote and unrealistic.

The railroad which proudly exhibited a map of the coal fields in its *Annual Report* for 1900, showing fifteen active anthracite breakers and several mine branches to serve them, now had only one sure source of colliery revenue—the solitary structure north of Scranton. The veins of premium coal were playing out and customers began to complain of the poor quality of O&W coal. Train crews learned to be cautious of the roadbed

When O&W passengers grew scarcer, this 1905 Harlan and Hollingsworth coach was converted to a combination car, enabling it to serve until the end of the O&W story.

The third port connection, in addition to the facilities at Cornwall and Weehawken, was this coal trestle at Oswego. It came down during the extensive modernization of Trustee Lyford in 1941.

This abbreviated conveyance is an extra leaving Fallsburg Station during the hectic summer tourist season in the lower Catskills.

This trim little frame building was more than adequate for local business at Franklin Springs. More important to the railroad's economy were the bulk shipments of iron ore from the nearby mines.

south of Forest City, finding heaves and twists where abandoned mine supports had given way underground. One crew came close to perforation when the engine headlamp disclosed the end of an uprooted rail staring them in the face. The Scranton Branch had no other source of revenue; passenger service had been negligible and thus abandoned years before; milk traffic decreased as strip mining tore up the surrounding landscape.

When President Nuelle resigned on April 1, 1937, railroaders all along the line knew that the blow was about to fall. Nuelle had seen the fortunes of the Company change over the years since his employment as Assistant Engineer in 1907; now he accepted a position as head of the Lehigh Coal and Navigation Company. The year following he took the top post with the Delaware and Hudson Company. His success demonstrates once again that the O&W never lacked superior leadership, even in its plunge towards insolvency.

The Board of Directors of the New York, Ontario and Western Railway Company filed a petition for reorganization under Section 77 of the Bankruptcy Act on May 19, 1937. The six months' grace period on bond interest was past, real estate taxes were mounting up, and fixed obligations were beyond the ability of the Company to pay. Accordingly, on the next day, Judge Murray Hulbert of the United States District Court for the Southern District of New York, approved the petition. Having long been associated with transportation (he had been Director of the Port of the City of New York), the continuing supervision of this knowledgeable jurist was to be most fortunate in the years to come.

The man approved by the Interstate Commerce Commission to take over the trusteeship of the O&W was another professional engineer—Frederic E. Lyford. He came direct from a position of director of sales for the Baldwin Locomotive Works, having also served for ten years with the Lehigh Valley. Apparently in an effort to economize, the ICC disapproved the appointment of a co-trustee, Vincent Dailey, whose petition had been passed upon favorably by representatives of the bond holders and by the Court. Dailey's specialty was business development, as Lyford's was railroad operation. Advocates of the co-trustee plan saw the need of getting the collieries on a firm commercial basis once again, but a majority of the Commissioners felt that Dailey's appointment would be unjustified for such a small operation. A clear division was made between the mines and the railroad, with the supposition that the coal companies could work out their difficulties by themselves. Later events cast considerable doubt upon the wisdom of the decision.

If the theory is true that history is cyclical, that events have a way of repeating themselves, then the old Midland was back in operation. Within sight of greatness as a tight and secure little railroad empire, the O&W failed once again to live up to its billing. The hard work and huge investment in men, roadbed and equipment had paid off in small but encouraging profits, but mostly in dreams again. Everyone from section hand to investment banker had faith in the aging line. The vision of the old Midland was not dead; it had never died.

*Jim Shaughnessy*

No one could remain unconvinced of the natural beauty of O&W terrain after seeing this view near Apex, New York. By 1957, however, Mother Nature was also taking over the right-of-way.

# CHAPTER SEVEN

Trustee Lyford embarked on a vigorous program of economy measures and traffic solicitation. The coal situation was chaotic and Pennsylvania anthracite could no longer be the mainstay of the railroad's economy. The trustee's policy was to convert the specialist carrier into a hauler of general merchandise. The whole emphasis of O&W operation had to be changed, as one look at the flooded and bankrupt mines could show. The task was one requiring salesmanship, vision and executive ability.

One of the most distasteful of decisions to the new management was the one to cut down the work force. Fortunately for the morale of O&W employees, many oldsters were ready for retirement. This made the task seem less drastic, for by the simple expedient of not replacing pensioners, a considerable number of names was dropped from the rolls. Representative of this group was John P. Hawver, 70 years old, who retired in 1937 as a passenger trainman after fifty-one rich years with the railroad. During these years, Hawver served under thirty-six regular conductors, his last run on the *Ontario Express*. A farm boy from Andes, New York, he was one of a large segment of O&W employees who were recruited from the rural countryside, drawn by a deep admiration for the romantic life of iron, smoke and cinders. John P. Hawver died in May of 1959, his own life paralleling almost exactly the existence of the railroad he served so well.

Passenger trainmen were rapidly becoming an oddity on the Ontario line. During the winter off-season, Trains *1* and *2* were adequate to accommodate travelers between Weehawken and Walton. The summer brought out several additional trains, but each year the time-worn coaches seemed dingier and the service less attractive. To preserve as much of this seasonal revenue as possible, the company turned to the noted "streamstylist" of the 1930's, German-born Otto Kuhler. Having designed the sleek and handsome "Hiawathas" of the Milwaukee Road, Kuhler was also an expert on "budget rebuilds."

The O&W had only $10,000 with which to upgrade its passenger trains, but under this severe limitation, the designer accomplished wonders. Working closely with the Middletown shop forces, Kuhler transformed a fifteen-year-old veteran, engine *No. 405*, into a dramatic and colorful steam locomotive. He mixed brilliant hues of orange and maroon paint with which to garnish the boiler, drivers, cab and tender. With stainless steel and chromium plate, he emphasized the handrails, the bell, and by the addition of two narrow stainless steel bands around it, the stack. Sheet metal skirts were run along the running boards and a large panel placed between the pilot braces. On this panel the age-old Ontario and Western symbol appeared with the added flair of orange wings.

Turning to necessary car renovations, Kuhler carried through the maroon color scheme with a horizontal stripe of light orange just below the windows, to suggest speed and motion. The interior appearance of the coaches was not only antiquated but shabby. To hide the soiled and worn seat cushions, tan slipcovers were made, with the railroad's monogram applied in a cool green. The walls were brightened with brushstrokes of gray and ivory paint, trim of black and maroon. Then, taking one of the steel parlor cars (the *Ulster*) of vintage 1913, the renovators laid new gray linoleum, threw out the old wicker armchairs, brought in inexpensive maple armchairs and wisely kept the rich mahogany paneling. The sister parlor-observation car, the

*Orange*, received similar treatment and soon the train stood in the Middletown yard, gleaming in the sunlight.

As an economy job, the *Mountaineer* was a model for other railroads to follow. Even the train crews wore maroon shirts and black trousers with a maroon stripe. It was unfortunate that air-conditioning was too costly for the O&W. The Middletown office staff doubled as models for its first publicity photos for the same reason. Then, just before Memorial Day, the *Mountaineer* stamped proudly out of the shops with Bob Hirst at the throttle and Walt Davis on the left-hand side. From the terminal at Middletown to the junction at Cadosia, she was the object of favorable comment from trackside observers.

Glamorizing was no real answer to the worsening situation of railroads throughout the United States. Some of the Ontario's neighbors found themselves counted among ICC statistics on abandonments. The Lehigh Valley connection near Sylvan Beach was severed in 1938, leaving the Fish Creek interlocking tower just another superfluous building. Originally the Canastota Northern, this line to Camden had little excuse for existence except the vacation trade to Oneida Lake, now gone. Further down the Northern Division, the Chenango Branch of the West Shore line vanished, excepting a few miles through Manlius. Thus, the junction at Earlville, long a transfer point for the Chicago trains, became a memory. That curious transportation anachronism, the Delaware and Northern, lasted longer than her revenues could justify. The D&N stopped running in 1942, deserting its singletrack between the O&W depot at East Branch and Arkville on the old Ulster and Delaware. The changing pattern of freight and passenger traffic affected every railroad company, including the O&W.

In 1939 the Company contemplated abandonment of some of its own unprofitable trackage. Two lines in particular were in danger—the Delhi and Monticello branches. The seventeen miles from Walton to Delhi still retained one mixed train daily except Sunday, but the Monticello station saw only special

Switcher *#52* had only a few more years of activity when this shot was taken at Norwich in 1941. The diesel revolution was just around the corner.

With a heavy Mountain type on the lead, the rumbling boxcars behind, freight trains like this soon became the principal source of O&W income.

Embellished with gleaming paint and polished metal, "streamstyled" *405* and her renovated coaches made a striking impression on employees and passengers alike.

The *Roscoe Express* eases out of Weehawken on a misty day in July of 1938.

children's camp trains in the summer and light local freights. The Delaware and Hudson was encouraged to foreclose its mortgage on the Utica and Rome branches, in order that short-line operation might relieve the O&W of financial responsibility while continuing to act as a feeder.

With coal tonnage down by almost half in 1939, the railway looked to bridge traffic as a means of support. Boxcar freight was solicited by the freight agents for transfer from the West to New England points. By dint of hard selling, the Lyford admin-istration achieved a tremendous increase in such revenues. When Lyford left his post in 1944, the item called "manufactur-ing and miscellaneous commodities" had multiplied from 17% of total tonnage to 50%.

Very little could be done about the uneven load distribution by which the O&W had few back loads. The railroad was pri-marily a receivers' line, with coal companies, feed mills, and construction outfits predominant. These patrons never supplied a carload on the return trip to the car's point of origin. Industry on the O&W was small and sparse. Besides this disadvantage, the company had no revenue-producing box cars of its own. The fifty-eight wooden rattlers still able to creak over the rails in 1939 were not fit for use in interchange traffic with other lines. Even the coal cars were antiques, ranging in age from 18 to 30 years.

Luckily for the plans to convert O&W to a bridge route, the roadbed and structures were in good condition. For almost fifty years the Company had expended large sums to maintain its track and bridges for anticipated dense and heavy traffic, which materialized with the coal boom and vanished when the mines failed. Nevertheless, as unneeded rails and ties were torn up, they were found in such good condition that they could be used elsewhere as replacements.

Several miles of such trackage were removed on the section from Cadosia to East Branch, where double track reverted to a single line, including Hawks Mountain Tunnel (which had

In its new livery, the old parlor car was a dramatic answer to the problem of dwindling passenger revenues.

Maple chairs, linoleum and bright colors transformed the *Ulster* from outdated gentility to updated luxury.

always been wide enough for but one train). Automatic signals were placed here as well as at the portals to Fallsburg and Bloomingburg (High View) Tunnels. This meant that towermen formerly located at each end night and day could be eliminated. Eighteen men became victims of technological unemployment.

To the general public these far-reaching alterations to the daily life of the railroad were not readily apparent. Their reaction to employee reductions and to other visible evidences of poverty was simple enough. They just shook their heads in amusement and joked about the "Old and Weary." The riders of the hump-backed old coaches which shuttled them into the Catskill resorts began calling their accommodations the "Great Timber Fleet," a quite appropriate description. On summer weekends the Middletown Station was a scene out of the past. Passenger trains ran in several sections, each holding a miscellany of human shapes and sizes—all hungry, thirsty and tired. They descended upon the lunch counter like ants on a lump of sugar. Then they entrained once more, and if at holiday time, they might be privileged to ride a steel New Haven, New York Central, Jersey Central or Reading passenger car. In the early days these O&W patrons might easily have sunk into Florida East Coast plush, for the two railroads had a very practical mutual assistance arrangement in the heyday of travel by rail. It would be hard to convince the crowded and hot human cargo aboard these trains that the O&W was going broke.

And yet this was so. The Interstate Commerce Commission in March of 1940 heard the first reorganization plan submitted by the Trustee and declined approval. The Company had not demonstrated that it could place itself on a sound financial footing. As more and more furnaces, both domestic and industrial, converted from anthracite to fuel oil, O&W income for transporting this commodity fell. Further cutbacks in maintenance and personnel expenses could not erase the everlasting deficit.

*page 146*

The *Mountaineer* went into action during the summer season of 1938. Here she is caught by the lens near Winterton in 1939.

This tower at the north portal of High View Tunnel was replaced in the economy drive by automatic signals.

New efforts were made to make the railway solvent once again. One unprofitable part of the system was neatly eliminated when the New Berlin Branch (including the 7-mile Wharton Valley Railroad) was sold to the Unadilla Valley short line for $25,000.00. Negotiations with the New York, Susquehanna & Western (once the New Jersey Midland) resulted in a joint operating arrangement, which was expected to produce operating economies. Five diesel-electric locomotives of 44 tons and 380 h.p. entered the motive power roster in 1941 and 1942. These were assigned to switching duties as they arrived and made impressive records for operating economy. The hoped-for sale and short-line operation of the Utica, Clinton & Binghamton fizzled, and instead, the O&W purchased the branch outright, at a cost of $1,200.00 per mile. Included in the sale was the 13-mile Rome and Clinton Railroad Company. Assessments of railroad property for taxing purposes were reduced about two-thirds after some conferences with O&W town representatives.

The activity centering on the offices in Middletown and in New York staggered the imagination. If the railway could be put upon a self-sustaining basis at all, the hard-thinking and honest efforts of the administration and the employees would do it. The majority of the members of the Ontario and Western family were veterans who had known better days on the railroad, for low-seniority men had been laid off as the company tightened its belt. Loyalty and cooperation among the railroaders seemed much better than might be expected under the depressing uncertainties of the times.

Better relations with the shipping public were encouraged by appointment of more freight representatives, expansion of a truck pickup-and-delivery service (begun at Liberty as early as 1932), and publication of a Company magazine, the *Ontario and Western Observer*. Illustrated brochures and colorful paper advertising items came streaming out of the main offices to the stations and the shippers along the line. The road attempted to give a more personal touch to its service by inventing a bandy-legged, moon-faced little man, fashioned from the letters "O" and "W", and christened, sure enough, "Owen W."

For one segment of the public, the O&W had irresistible appeal. In great numbers the railroad hobbyists "discovered" the struggling old pike through the center of New York State. With its antiquated cars, its ancient engines, its little rural depots, its unique natural setting and its valiant fight to stay alive, the "Old and Weary" captured the hearts of thousands of railroad fans in all parts of the country. Beginning in 1939 the number and size of fan trips—to Monticello, to Sidney, to Cornwall, and to all points—reached phenomenal proportions. World War II added other excursionists to the passenger consist of the O&W, and special trains went rambling up and down the main stem in a reenactment of the railroad's peak years. Sylvan Beach dwellers became accustomed to visiting firemen and factory employees entering the streets from the direction of the old passenger depot. The Hudson River steamer "Peter Stuyvesant" loaded sightseers from loaded trains at Cornwall for a combined rail-water excursion. A football train operated from Kenwood to Hamilton for the Colgate-Holy Cross game, chartered by Oneida Community, Limited, the business organization remnant of the religious experiment known as Perfectionism. This trip was a complete reversal of the Midland days, when the railway ran special trains to carry the curious to observe the workings of its communal arrangements (which included marriage). This 1941 journey was reminiscent of the Midland in one other way; before the string of cars could rattle safely back to Kenwood Station, the train broke in two. Fortunately for the passengers, a well-stocked "club car," set up in a combination coach, made the delay less tedious.

Delay of disaster proportions occurred on the line in May of 1942. Traffic on the Scranton Division halted indefinitely while maintenance-of-way crews surveyed the flood damage and began the colossal task of removing earth slides and filling in washouts. The destruction to all portions of O&W lines was so great that many observers stated flatly that the railroad was finished for all time. One full week of work restored the Scranton line to single-track operation, while other repairs to the main line were completed in two days. With its working force solidly backing it, the O&W refused to die.

New life appeared on the line with the rumbling of fast symbol freight trains connecting with similar hotshots of the Lackawanna, Lehigh Valley, New Haven, and Jersey Central. As this business mounted and coal movements subsided, the main line from Cadosia north and from Campbell Hall south became less and less important. Boxcar freight soon amounted to almost half of the tonnage on the O&W line. The war accounted for a great increase in this East-West traffic and placed more power at the tail end of Scranton Division freight trains.

Despite this welcome addition to O&W income, wartime demands on the railroad were disappointing. The operating ratio (of operating expenses to total operating revenues) was much too high. It rose from 89 in 1941 to 99.75 in 1945.

With its income base greatly broadened, including now such diverse traffic as merchandise bridge traffic, steel and iron from Pittsburgh for the East, eggs from New Berlin, newsprint from Canada, bauxite from South America to Canada and excursionists for all points, the O&W seemed on its way to recovery. At this juncture in its fortunes, Trustee Lyford resigned, and within a year, World War II came to an end.

1945 was the year in which the net operating loss topped the one million dollar mark. The new trustees, Raymond L. Gebhardt and Ferdinand J. Sieghardt, had accepted no easy task. As a first step they arranged the purchase of five diesel-electric locomotives from the Electro-Motive Division of General Motors. Gebhardt was an experienced Lehigh Valley Railroad official who had assisted Lyford's O&W efforts, and he saw the rugged, economical diesel units as the answer to

*page 150*

high operating costs. For this purpose, the Reconstruction Finance Corporation took over two million dollars' worth of Equipment Trust Certificates. The days of steam on the "Old and Weary" were numbered.

In three years the conversion from aging and ailing steam engines to gleaming, multi-colored diesels was accomplished. But not before steam had a brief minor triumph in 1947. A brisk rise in shipments over the line—amounting to almost a million dollars increase over 1946—sent officials scurrying around to dig up motive power to move this unexpected bounty. Five rusting hulks on the "strawberry patch" (scrap tracks) were pulled out just short of the cutting torch and their fires relighted for another run. The neighboring Delaware and Hudson likewise sold an old Mother Hubbard to the O&W. For a time the unlikely yoking of smoke-belching, snorting old steamers and flashy, moaning diesel streamliners could be seen rushing over the Southern Division. But in a few all-too-short months, O&W steam would be gone.

With steam went a great railroad tradition. The drama and excitement inherent in the sight of busy little Consolidations digging into the winding grades to the north, sometimes four and five strong, with rolling gray-black smoke illuminated by the orange light from yawning firebox doors, screaming for dirt-road crossings and hammering by into the dusk, such a soul-satisfying pageant was past. The thrill of watching a long string of gently-weaving boxcars rolling north from Mayfield, led by a heavy Mountain type and tailed by two ugly, snorting Santa Fe's, receded into fond memories. Although railfaring men were as proud of the murmuring diesel units as the trackside admirers were impressed, nothing could really replace the magical chant of steam.

Many of the veteran engineers had retired before the slick and immaculate motive power came on the road. Lew Eaton grasped the hand rails of *No. 308*, the Oneida yard engine, for the last time in 1941, ending fifty years of railroading. In the

*Jack Farrell*

Two beefy Santa Fe's give train *SU-1* a boost up the hill to Poyntelle on the symbol freight's run from Scranton to Utica in 1939.

While his engine is being coupled to train *37*, the *Ontario Express*, skull-capped Pat Diver checks his pocket watch, anxious to roll out of Middletown.

*Jack Farrell*

*Jack Farrell*

Special trains to the children's camps near Monticello brought out the aging wooden coaches, coupled to Engines *246* and *251,* on July 1, 1939.

In the late 1930's the O&W still handled milk traffic and the first and third cars of this Scranton-bound freight give evidence of it.

*Jack Farrell*

latter days of sharp union division of labor, Lew was notable for his affection and care for his engine, looking upon her as a friend and not as a machine to be run for eight hours and then abandoned. Pat Diver left the right-hand side in 1943, during the last days of regular passenger service. He had come a long way from his firing days on the Oneida pusher, for his last runs were on *Nos. 1* and *2*, managing one of the "Teakettles" or streamstyled *405*. His friendly wave, the tossed gifts of candy to little friends, and his black skull cap (which earned him the nickname "Rabbi") made his appearance at the cab window both notable and neighborly. And Homer House was an exception to the general rule that a man not work past the age of 65—instead, he put in 65 years as an O&W employee, 54 of them as an engineer, and quit only because the railroad itself stopped in 1957. His devotion to duty is an example that the present generation might well try to emulate. These men and thousands like them stood for the finest principles of old-time railroading. They were men and they were railroad men, with all that both names signify.

Dieselization put unaccustomed power in the hands of engine crews; one crew could now control a train which formerly needed two or more locomotives. The effect of such efficiency could be foreseen. Over a relatively short period of adjustment, the number of O&W employees dropped to less than half of what it had been in steam operation. The gradual decline in traffic volume was also a contributing factor to this reduction. Having weathered the very dark days of bankruptcy, the workers were confronted with further layoffs, an indication of darker days to come. Employee morale, which had continued at a surprisingly high level over the uncertain decade of bankruptcy, sank.

Beginning on April 18, 1949, not a train moved on the New York, Ontario & Western Railway. A strike by the operating brotherhoods threw everyone out of work except the officials; the Company could not afford to pay salaries with no current income. Organized labor argued that nationwide rail workers' raises had not been paid on the O&W. The Company maintained that as a corporation in trusteeship, it was not bound by national agreements. Besides, they said, we cannot pay more wages and stay in business. Federal mediation began at once, only to be interrupted by the sensational announcement that the paychecks just out were short by 15½ cents an hour. When the last wage agreement had been made in 1947, the O&W managers reserved the right to omit the increase when income was insufficient. The reason was clear, but the timing was off. No move could have created a worse effect on the strikers. Even when the Trustees promised to make up the deductions (on advice from Judge Conger, successor to Judge Hulbert) since the treasury was now adequate for the payment, bitterness remained.

Shortly after the beginning of the work stoppage, the two managers took another step which hardly endeared them to their employees. They petitioned the Court for complete abandonment of the line. Later the motion was clarified to show that the sale would not be for scrap, but for continued operation under a new owner. Nevertheless, O&W men felt that the top brass had tried to sell them out.

When tempers cooled on each side, a six months' truce was declared in which an objective expert could examine the property to determine whether the railroad might be operated in a more efficient manner. When the *Kiernan Report* appeared some months later it was a bombshell hurled into the quarrel. He accused the Trustees of lack of interest and ability necessary to run the road. Further, Mr. Kiernan recommended resignation of one of the two and the complete elimination of the other position.

The Trustees returned a blistering answer accusing the "unbiased observer" of seeking the top post for himself. They cited errors of fact and judgment which revealed a superficial, if not misleading, analysis of operating problems. Further, they drew

*George Phelps Collection*

At the junction at Randallsville, northbound train *#9* clears the main for a southbound freight, a midwinter scene now erased from the landscape.

The *Roscoe Express* blasts into Middletown with *282* and *227* on the lead and thirteen cars behind, including eight wooden coaches and the parlor car *Chenango*.

*Jack Farrell*

Train #9 waits for the highball at Walton in the warm noonday sun of a day in June of 1940. The milk business was already slipping away to more flexible motor trucks.

This scene of ticklish repair work was repeated all along the Scranton line in 1942 when spring floods knocked out service for a full week.

a conclusion which Kiernan had not emphasized. Even he implied that earnings were much too low at the time for any wage increases. Much of what the report outlined was already evident to employees, shippers and the Trustees themselves.

For example, Kiernan stated that "Public relations are at the lowest ebb and labor relations are at the contempt stage." Allowing for a certain amount of exaggeration, this remark was not far from the truth. The psychological distance between labor and management was greater at this time than it had ever been. As O&W finances became more and more entangled, legal procedures more complicated and traffic solicitation more desperate, top officials were seen less and less by the men. Objections to the remoteness of the Trustees are found in frequent references to "unnecessary" New York offices. Former presidents and high officers always had time for a chat with a station agent or a hostler. Among their fast friends were people they had worked beside before they were promoted. The new officials were all imposed upon the company by the Court and the ICC; they had few personal contacts with the men and little time in which to establish good relations.

Labor relations were certainly bad, and public relations were not much better. After many communities had cut O&W assessments in order to qualify for installment payments on tax bills, they discovered that even the small installments were soon omitted. Economy measures like abandonment of the Port Jervis and Monticello branch or cutbacks in passenger service were hard-fought battles in which the patrons usually won. The public felt that it had a substantial investment in the form of unpaid taxes by the company, and they resisted attempts to remove this asset from their towns. Shippers became antagonistic towards the line because of poor service, usually caused by the constant turnover of regular train crews, due to layoffs and subsequent "bumping" of lower-seniority employees. Unfamiliar workers made mistakes, and these were repeated as crews rotated. There seemed to be no way out.

*page 158*

Sam Rosoff saw a way out, and the clouds over O&W disappeared during the winter of 1949. The millionaire New York City subway magnate made a complete tour of the railroad in old *Car 30*, newly painted in orange, gray and yellow to match its diesel companions. For three days he inspected the line, met reporters, questioned the trustees who accompanied him, made encouraging speeches and assured all that he would place a bid for the property when it came up for sale in 1950. Having run the Delaware and Northern as a losing proposition until he sold it to the City of New York for a dam site, Rosoff was accustomed to making losses turn into profits. His influence with industry would undoubtedly bring new factories to locations along the line. For the first time in years, both employees and officials could smile and breathe sighs of relief. But like the old Midland, the Ontario and Western was doomed to disappointment.

The net loss for 1949 had been two million dollars in spite of all that could be done to reduce it. When the road went on the auction block in 1950, a disturbing new factor was present. The Federal Government entered the proceedings on account of nonpayment of Railroad Retirement taxes. The two bids which were submitted at the time were much too low, in the opinion of Judge Conger and Trustees Gebhardt and Sieghardt. Nothing was heard from Mr. Rosoff.

The agitation brought a new organization into being, however. The "Eleven-County Consolidated Committee" set out to boost the railroad out of debt with a cooperative effort of shippers. A retired coal dealer of Hamilton, New York, James E. Leland, was elected chairman. He was assisted by W. C. VanDuzer of Middletown and Professor William Kessler of the Department of Economics at Colgate University. Under their new slogan, "Now Young, Out, and Working," the businessmen cooperated in a venture to restore the body of the Old and Weary to health. Not even the earnest and energetic efforts of these men were enough. The deficit in 1951 was about the same.

Dr. Kessler, an ardent railroad buff as well as an authority on transportation economics, contributed to this muddled situation one of the most clear-headed surveys of the railroad's problems and potentialities. He based his presentation upon the hard facts that the O&W was in competition with stronger carriers at all large traffic centers (for its very own, it could claim only such villages as Walton, Delhi, Monticello, Liberty and Roscoe), that it originated very little traffic (therefore depending to a large extent upon deliveries from other lines), that union agreements worked a hardship upon it (a full-time hostler at Oswego turned the one locomotive that visited there each day) and that constant talk of abandonment kept industry from settling on the line (even those already there moved in late years). Dismissing impractical plans for breaking the road up into short lines to escape the expenses of New York State's Full Crew Act (mandating that on railways of over fifty miles in length a crew of six men be the minimum for a twenty-five car freight), he made three proposals. First of all, the continued operation of the O&W must be assured in order to attract shippers, restore the workers' sense of security, and acquire a firmer standing with other railroads. Secondly, he suggested that employees should have better knowledge of management affairs, which might be accomplished by transfer of main offices to Middletown. The third point mentioned had to do with reduction of expenses and improvement of traffic volume. Here the most important item was acquisition of Company cars to help equalize the heavy per diem payments (rental for car use) to other carriers.

By this time the Ontario and Western affair was a legal quagmire. Holders of O&W securities, the railroad unions, many counties, villages and cities and other individuals appeared before the court to protect their considerable, and in some cases, conflicting interests. Bondholders were anxious to liquidate the Company assets so that they could get the cash before further deterioration occurred. The Brotherhoods wanted

*Wilson Jones*

The smooth, clean diesel power assigned to passenger runs could not compete with the private automobile nor could it replace the dramatic steamer. The summer of 1952 brought such service to an end.

Dispatcher H. T. Dixon had control over the entire railroad, including the CTC sector below East Branch.

*Jim Shaughnessy*

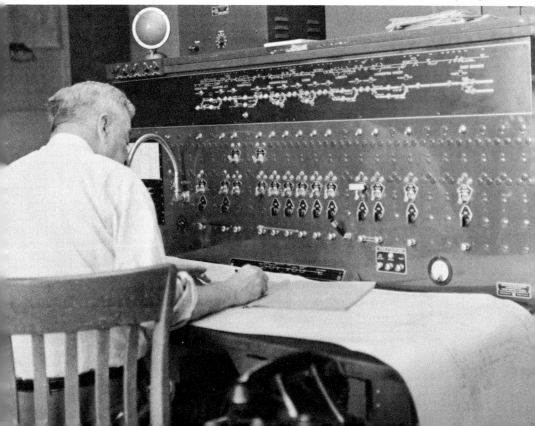

retroactive pay increases and, at the same time, continued operation. Governmental units were impatient at not getting back taxes and cared little for the method devised. The Federal Government, tolerant for a time of lack of payment of retirement and withholding taxes, became restive. The diminishing pressure group of shippers and receivers found its voice so weak that it was almost lost in the hullabaloo.

No longer were the protests against passenger service cuts loud and long. Elimination of the winter schedule hardly raised a ripple of discontentment, and O&W varnish rolled only from late May to early September. Delhi had already lost its traditional mixed train to the bus lines, and freight service only was on the way, coming in 1953. Autos and buses on improved Catskill highways hummed by the dilapidated little passenger stations on the now single-track main line. Not even the modernity of Centralized Traffic Control (dispatching by push button and toggle switch) could make up for the loss of its picturesque steam-powered, wooden-coached passenger trains.

O&W hopes rose once again in 1952. The New York, New Haven and Hartford Railroad made a cash offer to purchase the entire property. However, this offer of six and one-half million dollars was on New Haven terms, not on O&W stipulations (which included operation of the whole line for not less than five years from date of sale). The arrangements collapsed early in 1953 when the New Haven withdrew its bid because transfer of the property was required within thirty days. This impatience lacked sincerity, though, and a more likely reason could be found in the financial troubles of the New Haven. But O&W morale dropped again.

Other bids to buy, with provisions to scrap certain portions, operate others for specified periods and fulfill various other requirements were numerous during the next two years. Finally, in February of 1954, Judge Conger came to the conclusion that he and the Trustees had no right to sell the road under the law, and that reorganization was the single authorized procedure. At this juncture, Trustee Sieghardt resigned, his partner having died in 1953.

The new head of the declining Company was 70-year-old Lewis D. Freeman, the last Chief of the Railroad Division of the Reconstruction Finance Corporation. The year before his appointment, the RFC had attempted to reclaim the diesel loco-motives, and thus Freeman changed sides. He faced a situation demanding not only administrative ability, but also a good deal of courage. Freight originated and terminated on the O&W was down to 183,000 tons per year, as against 4,611,000 in 1936; almost 50% of all revenues came from overhead, or bridge, traffic. Therefore, greatest attention was given to the expansion of the freight solicitation forces in major cities.

On December 1, 1954, the Trustee submitted a reorganiza-tion plan recommending sale to the Pinsley group, short-line railroad operators, for $4,600,000 (identical with the cost of bailing out the Midland in 1880). The contract carried a com-mitment on the part of the buyer to operate the main line for at least ten years. However, the Pinsley purchase agreement was predicated upon a report by railroad analysts who thought abandonment of parts of the main line might be necessary. The ICC considered that the ten year stipulation was likely to be inoperative, and also heard the complaints of bondholders whose claims would not be covered by the purchase price. A plan which the bondholders proposed involving piggy-back transport between Cornwall and Oswego had not, in the words of the Commission, "got much beyond the stage of wishful think-ing." Both plans were dismissed as impractical late in 1956 and it was recommended that the Court should terminate the bank-ruptcy proceedings. "No plan of reorganization can be formu-lated and approved, either now or in the foreseeable future."

The Ontario and Western was in trouble with Uncle Sam. The Federal Government opposed any reorganization attempts and encouraged liquidation. This change of heart came shortly

Jim Shaughnessy

The massive old station at Middletown soon saw only passing freights, such as *NE-6*, led by fuel-experimental engine #601, given to the railroad for almost nothing at the end of Esso tests.

Charles Diebold

Far from home, the famed "honeymoon car," painted to match diesel equipment stands at Buffalo after her purchase by Mr. Charles Diebold.

after public acknowledgement that the Company had not been meeting its obligations to pay withholding and retirement taxes for its employees. Embarrassing questions were asked in the halls of Congress, and the lawmakers quickly understood that indignant taxpayers outnumbered the friends of the O&W by a large margin. Consequently, Judge Conger reluctantly turned over the affairs of the railway to Judge Sylvester Ryan and Receivers James Kilsheimer and Jacob Grumet. Judge Ryan gave the new appointees sixty days to put the railroad back in the black, using voluntary loans from a grass-roots campaign to keep the road running. Almost $250,000 came in to meet current expenses, but in spite of a great reduction of running expenses, the funds ran out and operation ceased on March 29, 1957.

A shocked New York State Legislature passed a one million dollar aid bill to keep the O&W running as essential to civil defense. This dramatic gesture remained only a gesture, for the disapproval of the State Civil Defense Commission sealed the fate of the Old and Weary. Outcries from the unions and shippers' groups had little effect except for sympathetic noises from their political representatives. And so, in July of 1957, the 544-mile pike was auctioned off piecemeal for ten million dollars.

The New York and Oswego Midland was born in an atmosphere of bitterness and controversy; the New York, Ontario and Western died in the midst of turmoil and dissension. Somehow the personality of the long-suffering railroad came through as the most admirable of them all. Weak and neglected, attacked by all the devices known to man and nature, the old lady outlasted every one. Her passing was mourned for a variety of economic and sentimental reasons, but the loss was deeply felt in an intangible way. The rambling, elderly, inefficient, accident-prone, irritating old railroad was a part of a way of life now gone from the American scene.

Ravaged by the scrap dealers, the weed-covered old right-of-way is an ugly scar on the land. May it ever remind us of the days of glory when smoke plumes rose over rattling coaches, when iron men piloted panting steamers over the mountains, when the railroad depot was the business center of town, when the lined face of an engineer could bring joy into the life of a small child, when the far-off whistle made dreamers of us all.

*George Phelps Collection*

Form T.D. 11-AA

# New York, Ontario and Western Railway

LEWIS D. FREEMAN, TRUSTEE

TRAIN ORDER NO. *24*                         *M'town Mar 29,* 19 *57*

To *C and E Eng 805*     At *Norwich*

X..................................................Operator                         ..................................M.

*Eng 805 Run Extra*

*Norwich to Middletown.*

*J.B.Y.*

CONDUCTOR AND ENGINEMAN MUST EACH HAVE A COPY OF THIS ORDER

Made *Complete* Time *824* *P* M. *R. McElligott* Operator

*Robert F. Harding*

The last train order issued on the line was this commonplace sheet that formally ended O&W operation and consigned #805 to the auction block.

APPENDIX

ROSTER OF EQUIPMENT

T HE INFORMATION about New York, Ontario & Western steam motive power is almost wholly the work of Gerald M. Best, prominent railroad historian and author of *Minisink Valley Express* (the definitive history of the O&W's Port Jervis and Monticello line), with certain additional information supplied in footnotes. The mechanical data is contained in the line preceding each group of locomotives, in this fashion: the first number gives the outside diameter of the driving wheels including tires, the second lists cylinder measurements (diameter and stroke), the third is the total weight of engine in pounds, the fourth is the weight on the driving wheels, the fifth shows the boiler pressure and the sixth is the tractive effort. In certain cases, missing figures have been furnished by S. O. Kimball of Flint, Michigan. Where no figure is given, no official data is available.

The roster of motor cars and of official and parlor cars which follows the steam locomotive list has been supplied by John Stellwagen of Goshen, New York, who has compiled a complete roster of O&W passenger equipment.

The diesel roster is based upon the extensive listing compiled by Sterling O. Kimball, with some rearrangement and additions by the author. In updating disposition data, the work of Edward G. Koehler for the *Ontario & Western Observer* has been especially helpful. Wherever possible, information has been taken from or checked against official company records. Specifications are listed in this order: wheel diameter, drive arrangement, total weight, tractive effort and horsepower.

# THE STEAM LOCOMOTIVES OF THE NEW YORK, ONTARIO & WESTERN RAILWAY

First numbering – Lettered N.Y. & O.M. when purchased

Dimensions:
1- 7  60 – 17x22 – 64000
8-12  60 – 17x20 – 64000
13-14  60 – 14x22 – 56000
15-18  60 – 17x22 – 64000

| No. | TYPE | BUILDER, BUILDER'S No. | NAME | DATE | DISPOSITION |
|---|---|---|---|---|---|
| 1 | 4-4-0 | Rhode Is. #101 | Oswego | 4/1869 | Sold to N.Y. Loco. Works 10/27/1887. Scr. 1/1888 |
| 2 | 4-4-0 | Rhode Is. #102 | Madison | 4/1869 | Sold to N.Y. Loco. Works 10/22/1887. Resold to Centralia & Chester RR 4/1888 |
| 3 | 4-4-0 | Rhode Is. #103 | Chenango | 4/1869 | Sold to N.Y. Loco. Works 10/24/1887. Resold to Centralia & Chester RR 4/1888 |
| 4 | 4-4-0 | Rhode Is. #109 | Delaware | 5/1869 | Sold to Carthage & Adirondack RR 9/19/1887 |
| 5 | 4-4-0 | Rhode Is. #110 | Sullivan | 5/1869 | Sold to N.J.&N.Y.R.R. 4/1886 |
| 6 | 4-4-0 | Rhode Is. #120 | Otsego | 8/1869 | Sold 10/23/1886 |
| 7 | 4-4-0 | Rhode Is. #121 | Orange | 8/1869 | Sold prior 1880 |
| 8 | 4-4-0 | Rhode Is. #124 | Oneida | 9/1869 | Scrapped 1/18/1887 |
| 9 | 4-4-0 | Rhode Is. #125 | Ulster | 9/1869 | Sold to N.Y. Loco. Works 10/22/1887. Resold to Centralia & Chester RR 4/1888 |
| 10 | 4-4-0 | Rhode Is. #126 | Fulton | 9/1869 | Scrapped 9/24/1887 |
| 11 | 4-4-0 | Rhode Is. #131 | Eaton | 9/1869 | Sold to N. Y. Loco. Works 10/4/1887. Scr. 1/1888 |
| 12 | 4-4-0 | Rhode Is. #132 | Oxford | 9/1869 | Sold to N. Y. Loco. Works 10/24/1887. Scr. 1/1888 |
| 13 | 4-4-0 | Rhode Is. #135 | Norwich | 10/1869 | Sold prior 1874 |
| 14 | 4-4-0 | Rhode Is. #134 | New Berlin | 10/1869 | Sold to C.M.&St.P. 6/1881 |
| 15 | 4-4-0 | Rhode Is. #185 | De Ruyter | 6/1870 | Sold to N.Y. Loco. Works 10/25/87. Scr. 1/1888 |
| 16 | 4-4-0 | Rhode Is. #186 | Delhi | 6/1870 | Sold to N.Y. Loco. Works 10/24/87. Resold to Centralia & Chester RR 4/1888 |
| 17 | 4-4-0 | Rhode Is. #187 | Walton | 6/1870 | Sold to N.Y. Loco. Works 10/28/87. Scr. 1/1888 |
| 18 | 4-4-0 | Rhode Is. #188 | Constantia | 6/1870 | Sold to N.Y. Loco. Works 10/26/87. Resold to Centralia & Chester RR 4/1888 |

| No. | Type | Builder | Date | Name | Class/Dimensions & Notes |
|---|---|---|---|---|---|
| | | | | | 54 – 16x24 – 72000 |
| 19 | 2-6-0 | Rhode Is. #189 | 7/1870 | Stockbridge | Sold between 1890 and 1893 |
| 20 | 2-6-0 | Rhode Is. #190 | 8/1870 | Sidney | Sold 5/3/1887 |
| | | | | | 52 – 15x22 – 54000 |
| 21 | 0-4-0 | Rhode Is. #229 | 8/1870 | Ellenville | Sold to M. W. Dept. 12/29/1899. Used to push transfer table, Middletown. Retired 7/1903 |
| 22 | 0-4-0 | Rhode Is. #199 | 8/1870 | Ontario | Leased to Terminal Co. 1884. Later sold to them |
| | | | | | 54 – 16x24 – 72000 |
| 23 | 2-6-0 | Rhode Is. #297 | 7/1871 | Guilford | Traded to Sinnemahoning Valley RR with 1st 31, for S.V. #2 (NYO&W 2nd 89) 5/16/87 |
| 24 | 2-6-0 | Rhode Is. #298 | 8/1871 | Smyrna | Sold 5/31/1887 |
| 25 | 2-6-0 | Rhode Is. #299 | 8/1871 | Plymouth | Sold in 1887 |
| 26 | 2-6-0 | Rhode Is. #300 | 8/1871 | Volney | Sold to N.Y. Loco. Works 10/24/87. Resold to Centralia & Chester RR 4/1888 |
| 27 | 0-4-0 | Rhode Is. #301 | 9/1871 | Hudson | #27 52 – 15x22 – 54000. Renumbered 2nd 23 1/22/1889 |
| 28 | 0-4-0 | Rhode Is. #308 | 9/1871 | Clinton | #28 60 – 14x22 – 54000. Sold to C.M.&St.P. 6/1881 |
| | | | | | 61¾ – 17x22 – 72000 |
| 29 | 4-4-0 | Baldwin #2552 | 9/1871 | Sussex | Rebuilt at Cooke 6/1898 as 2nd 16 |
| 30 | 4-4-0 | Baldwin #2551 | 9/1871 | Minsink | Rebuilt at Cooke 10/1897 as 2nd 13 |
| *31 | 4-4-0 | Baldwin #2580 | 10/1871 | Neversink | Traded with 1st 23 for Sinnemahoning Valley #2 5/16/1887 |
| 32 | 4-4-0 | Baldwin #2579 | 10/1871 | Wallkill | Rebuilt at Cooke 12/1896 as 2nd 11 |
| | | | | | 54 – 17x24 – 74000 |
| 33 | 2-6-0 | Baldwin #2592 | 10/1871 | Franklin | Class L. Renumbered 2nd 54, 2/2/1889 |

• *Information recently furnished from old ledgers by Sterling O. Kimball indicates that #25 rather than #31 was the second engine involved in this trade. The evidence to support this point is strong enough to convince the author that this was the case. In the absence of reliable records from the period, no one can be absolutely certain.*

## THE STEAM LOCOMOTIVES OF THE NEW YORK, ONTARIO & WESTERN RAILWAY (Continued)

| No. | Type | Builder, Builder's No. | Date | Name | Disposition |
|---|---|---|---|---|---|
| 34-37, 39-42 | | | | | 61¾ – 17x24 – 90000 – 72000 |
| 34 | 4-4-0 | Baldwin #2614 | 11/1871 | Hackensack | Sold to Cooperstown & Charlotte Valley 2nd #4, 6/1900. Became D&H #416 9/19/03. Scrapped 4/20/1905 |
| 35 | 4-4-0 | Baldwin #2616 | 11/1871 | Shawangunk | Scrapped 1896 |
| 36 | 4-4-0 | Baldwin #2618 | 11/1871 | Middletown | Rebuilt at Cooke 8/5/96 as 2nd 10 |
| 37 | 4-4-0 | Baldwin #2643 | 12/1871 | Sandburgh | Rebuilt at Cooke 10/1897 as 2nd 14 |
| 38 | 4-4-0 | Baldwin #2646 | 12/1871 | Crawford | 38  56¾ – 12x22 – 48000  Class F; Renumbered 2nd 28, 2/2/1889 |
| 39 | 4-4-0 | Baldwin #2666 | 1/1872 | Mamakating | Scrapped 4/1900 |
| 40 | 4-4-0 | Baldwin #2668 | 1/1872 | Liberty | Rebuilt at Cooke 10/1897 as 2nd 15 |
| 41 | 4-4-0 | Baldwin #2692 | 2/1872 | Otselic | Renumbered 3rd 28, 11/7/1906 |
| 42 | 4-4-0 | Baldwin #2722 | 3/1872 | Pharsalia | Sold 1/7/1905 |
| 43 | 2-6-0 | Baldwin #2694 | 2/1872 | Preston | 54¾ – 17x24 – 74000  Class L; Renumbered 2nd 55 2/3/1889 |
| 44 | 4-4-0 | Baldwin #2724 | 3/1872 | McDonough | 61¾ – 17x24 – 72000  Class F; Scrapped 4/1900 |
| 45 | 2-6-0 | Baldwin #2782 | 4/1872 | Fallsburgh | 54¾ – 17x24 – 74000  Class L; Renumbered 2nd 56, 1/29/1889 |
| 46 | 0-4-0 | Baldwin #2783 | 4/1872 | Paterson | 54¾ – 15x22 – 68000; Renumbered 2nd 20, 1/27/1889 |
| 47 | 2-6-0 | Baldwin #2815 | 5/1872 | Dundee | 54¾ – 17x22 – 74000  Class L; Renumbered 2nd 53, 2/16/1889 |
| 48 | 2-8-0 | Baldwin #2840 | 6/1872 | Jersey City | 48 – 20x24; Sold prior 1880 |

| No. | Type | Builder | Date | Name | Notes |
|---|---|---|---|---|---|
| | | | | | 54 – 17x24 – 74000 Class L |
| 49 | 2-6-0 | Baldwin #2829 | 6/1872 | *Bloomingdale* | Sold to Scioto Valley RR #13, 6/1881. Became Norfolk & Western #523. Sold by them to Bower & Straus 2/1903 |
| 50 | 2-6-0 | Baldwin #2832 | 6/1872 | *Weehawken* | Scrapped 7/1/1906 |
| 51 | 2-6-0 | Baldwin #2872 | 7/1872 | *Newfoundland* | Scrapped 9/30/1908 |
| 52 | 2-6-0 | Baldwin #2929 | 9/1872 | *Ogdensburgh* | Scrapped 10/6/1908 |
| | | | | | 48 – 20x24 |
| 53 | 2-8-0 | Baldwin #2869 | 7/1872 | *Hamburgh* | Sold to DL&W(ML) #34, later 745-737-715 |
| | | | | | 61¾ – 17x24 – 72000 |
| 54 | 4-4-0 | Baldwin #2925 | 9/1872 | *Wawayanda* | Renumbered 2nd 33, 1/26/1889 |
| 55 | 4-4-0 | Baldwin #2964 | 10/1872 | *Hancock* | Renumbered 2nd 43, 1/28/1889 |
| 56 | 4-4-0 | Baldwin #2966 | 10/1872 | *Wantage* | Renumbered 2nd 38, 2/3/1889 |
| | | | | | 54 – 17x24 – 74000 Class L |
| 57 | 2-6-0 | Baldwin #3009 | 11/1872 | *Unionville* | Scrapped 10/1895 |
| 58 | 2-6-0 | Baldwin #3015 | 11/1872 | *Rockland* | Sold to New York & Penna. RR. 12/1899 |
| 59 | 2-6-0 | Baldwin #3083 | 1/1873 | *Hamden* | Rebuilt at Rome Mach. Wks. 1902 as #117 |
| 60 | 2-6-0 | Baldwin #3082 | 1/1873 | *Unadilla* | Sold to Sou. Iron & Equip. Co. #568 1/10/07. Resold to Florala Sawmill Co. #3, Paxton, Fla. 3/1/07. Traded back to SI&E 3/13/13. Resold to Louisiana Saw Mill Co. #50, Alexandria, La. |
| 61 | 2-6-0 | Baldwin #3096 | 1/1873 | *Monticello* | Rebuilt at Rome Mach. Wrks. 1902 as #119 |
| 62 | 2-6-0 | Baldwin #3097 | 1/1873 | *Wawarsing* | Rebuilt at Rome Mach. Wks. 1902 as #120 |
| 63 | 2-6-0 | Baldwin #3131 | 2/1873 | *Callicoon* | Rebuilt at Cooke 12/1898 as #116 |
| 64 | 2-6-0 | Baldwin #3130 | 2/1873 | *Lebanon* | Rebuilt at Rome Mach. Wks. 1902 as #121 |
| | | | | | 54 – 17x24 – 72000 |
| 65-67 | | | | | No locomotives in the NY&OM series. These numbers were vacant. |
| 68 | 2-6-0 | Rhode Is. #431 | 9/1872 | *Tompkins* | Renum. from 79 after delivery. Renumbered again to 2nd 78 in 1873 |

## THE STEAM LOCOMOTIVES OF THE NEW YORK, ONTARIO & WESTERN RAILWAY (Continued)

| No. | Type | Builder, Builder's No. | Date | Name | Disposition |
|---|---|---|---|---|---|
| 69 | 4-4-0 | Rogers #2053 | 1872 | *60 – 16x24*<br>Rip Van Winkle | Taken back by Rogers at Receiver's sale in 1874. (Had not been paid for) |
| | | | | 70-71 66 – 17x24 | 75-77 56 – 16x24 – 60000 |
| *70 | 4-4-0 | Rogers #1811 | 1870 | *72-74 54 – 16x24*<br>Passaic | Taken over by N. J. Midland 1874. To NYS&W #1 |
| 71 | 4-4-0 | Rogers #1856 | 1871 | C. A. Wortendyke | Taken over by N. J. Midland 1874. To NYS&W #2 |
| 72 | 4-4-0 | Rogers #1868 | 1871 | Pequannock | Sold to Middletown & Crawford RR #72, 1874 |
| 73 | 4-4-0 | Rogers | 1871 | Deckertown | Taken over by N. J. Midland 1874. To NYS&W #3 |
| 74 | 4-4-0 | Rogers | 1871 | Charlotteburg | Taken over by N. J. Midland 1874. To NYS&W #4 |
| 75 | 4-4-0 | McKay Iron Wks. | 10/1872 | Hamilton | Sold to Richmond & Potomac RR 6/1881 |
| 76 | 4-4-0 | McKay Iron Wks. | 10/1872 | Wawoiagin | Sold to Petersburg R.R. 6/1881 |
| 77 | 4-4-0 | McKay Iron Wks. | 12/1872 | Neskeglowitt | Sold to C.M.&St.P. 6/1881 |
| | | | | 54 – 17x24 – 72000 | |
| 78 | 2-6-0 | Rhode Is. #430 | 9/1872 | Courtland | Renumb. 2nd 68, 1873. Renamed Utica |
| 79 | 2-6-0 | Rhode Is. #431 | 9/1872 | Tompkins | Renumb. 1st 68, 1873, then 2nd 78. |
| 2nd 79 | 4-4-0 | Rogers | 1872 | Ramapo | Origin unknown. Sold to NJM #85. 1874 |
| | | | | 56 – 17x24 – 64000 | |
| 80 | 4-4-0 | Rhode Is. #432 | 10/1872 | Lansing | Renumb. 1st 66, 10/1887 |
| 81 | 4-4-0 | Rhode Is. #443 | 10/1872 | Genoa | Renumb. 1st 67, 10/1887 |
| 82 | 4-4-0 | Rhode Is. #444 | 10/1872 | Venice | Renumb. 2nd 69, 10/1/1887 |
| 83-84 | Vacant | | | | |
| 85 | 4-4-0 | Rhode Is. #531 | 6/1873 | Norwich | Returned to R. I. Wks. 1874. To NJM #80 – NYS&W #10 |

* Nos. 70-74 were originally New Jersey Midland engines, as their names would indicate, numbered 1-5. They were renumbered when the roads were connected. The "Passaic" was the locomotive scheduled to be named "Devitt C. Littlejohn."

| NEW YORK 225.14 | **NORWICH** | OSWEGO 99.66 |

Norwich was one of the larger cities served by the O&W. They had competition, initially from the Chenango Canal and later from the DL&W's Binghamton-Utica line. Although Sidney was the division point, the shops were at Norwich. Though they were smaller than the complex at Middletown, they were still quite respectable and had even produced one complete locomotive: a camelback 4-4-0 in 1898. When the first through freight service was introduced in 1927, it called for the O&W to handle trains from Maybrook to Norwich where they would be turned over to the Lackawanna to go west. The arrangement lasted only a short time before the connection was changed to Scranton, a somewhat shorter run. Norwich was the final holdout of steam and on July 21, 1948, the curtain rang down as the 402 rolled in from Sidney and dropped her fire, joining the line of sisters that were moved up to the DL&W connection for their last trip to the scrap

yard. Above, it's twilight once again, for the diesels that replaced the steamers were not the road's salvation. FT 805 is rolling north through the empty Norwich yards towards the freight house and station in the distance. It's March, 1957 and the end is only a few days away.

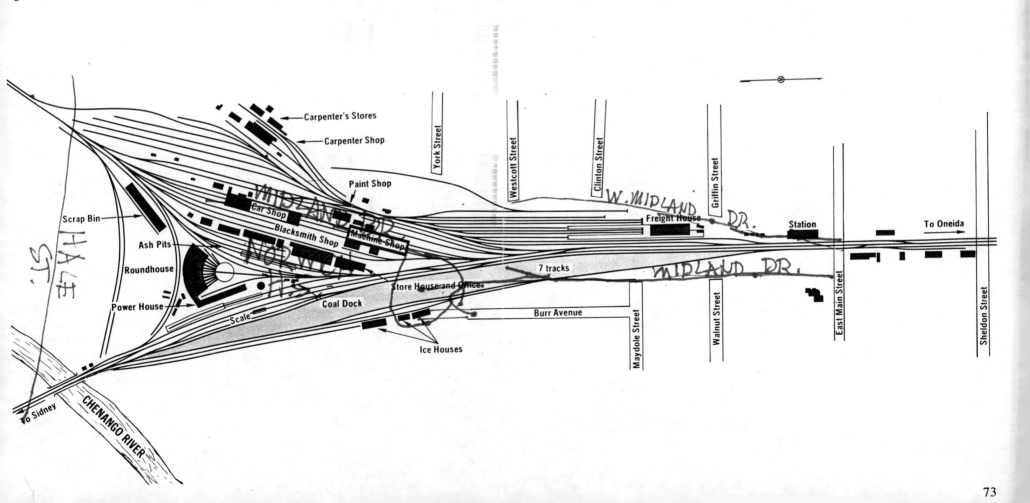

WILLIND AND DR

MIDLAND RR

MIDLAND RR

MIDLAND RR

NORWICH
R.R.

Hudsons, and Mohawks, and rarely an 0-6-0 or a Boston & Albany Berksh
welcome relief, shown above headed by Eng. 402. Home rails were still
four miles to the New York state line.

Below left, northbound Train No. 1 rolling through West Nyack, N.Y. five
line. West Shore tracks are drifting eastward back towards the Hudson and
will plunge into the 1620 ft. Haverstraw Tunnel and emerge near the wes
Hudson, Valley.

# A BRIEF HISTORICAL SKETCH

The O&W was born in the post-Civil War period; a time when the nation looked to territorial and industrial expansion to heal the wounds of internal warfare and reunification. The building of the transcontinental railroad perhaps best exemplified the sense of "manifest destiny" and inspired a host of less ambitious projects. Literally every village of any consequence felt that its future lay in a connection to the outside world over a road of iron rails on hand-hewn ties.

In October of 1865, a group of worthies gathered at Delhi in upstate New York to discuss the possibility of constructing a railroad from Oswego on Lake Ontario to the ports of New York. The principals were the Hon. Dewitt C. Littlejohn, former mayor of Oswego and then Speaker of the State Assembly, and Henry Low of Middletown, then a State Senator. There was much talk of an "air line" route until the more pragmatic matter of financing the new road came up. With the self-serving finesse that has made politician a dirty word, Littlejohn and Low rammed through a piece of legislation known as the Town Bonding Act, which allowed municipalities in the state to bond themselves for the construction of a railroad. This otherwise obscure piece of legislation would have a lasting effect on the newly formed New York & Oswego Midland, for their route wandered all over the state in an attempt to touch down on those communities which put up the proper amount of hard cash. Some hard-pressed New York taxpayers would have been quite indignant had they known that as late as 1970, they were still paying off some of these old Midland bonds. Unfortunately many of these villages would never fulfill the grand dreams they envisioned and the larger cities which already had

rail service would not commit tax dollars for still another line.

It took three years to hash out the meandering route and raise the money and the first spade of dirt was turned at Norwich in June, 1868. The construction proceeded with great difficulty, both in the field of engineering and finance. In typical nineteenth century fashion, however, the principals always collected a handsome salary no matter how anemic the treasury might be. After five years of ups and downs, the railroad was completed on July 9, 1873 and the next day saw the first through train from Oswego to Jersey City. The Midland itself terminated at Middletown, but had made arrangements to reach Jersey City via the New Jersey Midland. Initially the Oswego Midland had tied its fortunes to the New Jersey company, but later hard times would see the two go their separate ways. The New Jersey portion would become the New York, Susquehanna & Western while the segment from the state line to Middletown would eventually become the 14.5-mile Middletown & Unionville short line.

With typical Midland luck, the road was completed just in time for the Panic of 1873 and went into receivership the same month it was completed. The Receivers valiantly attempted to operate the line despite seizures of engines and rolling stock by irate tax collectors. After two years of incredible hardships their luck began to take an upward turn. The milk business which had begun as a single car in 1871 had grown to substantial proportions and the Centennial Exposition of 1876 added revenue dollars to the passenger accounts as New Yorkers flocked to Philadelphia to celebrate the nation's hundredth birthday. The road was up for sale and the black ink on the ledger books would not be ignored for long. It quickly attracted the attention of Conrad N. Jordan of New York, a banker representing some parties with an unusual interest in the Midland.

On November 14, 1879, Jordan bought the railroad for $4.6 million, a bargain basement price for a property that had cost a good $26 million to build. It seems in retrospect that his interest in the property was minimal and he was really acting as an agent for George Pullman and a number of associates who all shared a common dislike for Commodore Vanderbilt and his New York Central and Hudson River Railroad. Pull-

man had never forgiven Vanderbilt for using the sleeping cars of his arch-rival Wagner, and this was the chance to get even. He sent his vice-president Horace Porter off to New York to handle the project and his first task was to organize the New York West Shore & Buffalo. On January 21, 1880 the old Midland was resurrected as the New York Ontario & Western Railway and with the West Shore, jointly organized the North River Construction Company. The construction company was supposed to build the West Shore, utilizing some pieces of existing trackage and additionally build a branch for the O&W from Middletown to the Hudson River at Cornwall. It is futile to attempt to sort out the financial high-jinks of the three companies in the period from 1880 to 1885. The West Shore was built in fairly short order and the Ontario got their branch along with trackage rights to Weehawken and terminal facilities opposite New York. In the typical fashion of the period, the rich got richer (through stock manipulations) and the poor (the small shareholders) got measurably poorer, for the new West Shore got into a rate war with the New York Central. The well-established Central was more able to sustain this sort of blood-letting and eventually bought out the debilitated West Shore, strangely giving the O&W a very generous terminal and trackage rights agreement.

With the Pullman people gone and a new host of British and Dutch investors in their place, the Ontario proceeded to stake out its new place in the sun under the leadership of Thomas P. Fowler. The new president had come from a family with numerous railroad and steamship interests and the law school honors graduate had broken into the business as counsel to Vander-

bilt. If any single man can be credited with making something of the O&W, then it was certainly Fowler. He took the company from a run down ne'er-do-well and turned it into a first class carrier in all respects. His first year in office (1886) saw the lease of the Rome and Utica branches, originally short lines that had fallen under D&H control. His pet project, however, was the 54 mile Scranton division from Cadosia to Scranton which opened in 1890. Fowler knew that access to the coal fields of the Lackawanna valley would usher in a new era of prosperity and his forecast was correct. The new coal traffic put heavy demands on the railroad and Fowler poured huge amounts of capital into the plant, rebuilding and expanding facilities all along the line. At the same time the milk business and the passenger trade continued to grow; the O&W knew what salesmanship was all about and never missed an opportunity to promote any service that would add a dime to the bottom line.

By 1900 the O&W had acquired a substantial reputation among the New York area roads and that year they acquired the old Port Jervis Monticello & New York. Two years later the original line from Summitville to Ellenville was extended through to Kingston, giving the O&W the map it would retain until 1957. In 1904 the New Haven bought a controlling interest in the O&W for the apparent purpose of gaining leverage in their dealings with other roads. They could always threaten to use the Ontario to break out of their New England enclave. In the fall of 1912, President Fowler resigned and turned over the reins to his former vice-president John B. Kerr. The following year proved to be the peak for both passengers and milk and the O&W began, imperceptably at first, to decline towards insolvency.

The USRA operation during World War I left the O&W in poor shape and it took some time before the road began to enjoy the prosperity of a booming economy. Despite the good times, changes were being wrought. Improved state roads brought increased automobile ownership that was taking the customers out of the coaches in increasing numbers. The service cutbacks began in 1929 and by the early 1930's many parts of the road were freight only. The opening of new coal breakers in the Scranton area lifted coal tonnages to an all time high in 1932 and despite the depression, the O&W succeeded in paying dividends until 1935. The bottom dropped out rapidly as the mines began to play out after two generations of mining, and as strikes became more frequent. Gas and oil began to displace anthracite for home heating and coal tonnages fell rapidly. The final blow came in the spring of 1937 as two of the three company owned collieries failed. President Joseph H. Nuelle, who had succeeded Kerr in 1930, resigned and moved on to the D&H. The failure of the collieries caused the parent O&W to default on its bonds, and in lieu of a new president the O&W instead got themselves a court appointed trustee. On May 19, 1937 they filed Section 77 bankruptcy proceedings.

The job of saving the ailing road fell to Frederick E. Lyford, an experienced railroader who went to work trying to find new sources of income to replace the fading coal revenues. He attempted innovation in the passenger department and strived hard to capture for the O&W a share of the bridge traffic moving from the west to New England and Canada. The onset of World War II increased carloadings and perhaps served to mask the futility of Lyford's prodigious efforts. He resigned in 1944 and turned over the trustee's position to his former assistant Raymond L. Gebhardt and a new co-trustee, Ferdinand J. Sieghardt.

The team of Sieghardt and Gebhardt decided that salvation lay in a policy of dieselization and they pursued it until the last steamer was banished from the property in 1948. Passenger service was cut back progressively until September of 1953 saw the O&W join that growing number of roads in the Official Guide that carried the designation "Freight Service Only." The O&W's fortunes progressed from bad to worse in what has become a very familiar scenario, but which we must remember was unique at the time for a 500 mile Class 1 road. Labor relations degenerated after a 1947 strike with the O&W men working for substantially less than the national wage in an attempt to save their jobs. Shippers became increasingly dissatisfied with the serv-

ice and many connecting roads would not route a car O&W unless the bill was prepaid, assuring them of their share of the rate. Trustee Gebhardt died in 1953 and his partner resigned the following year, with the court naming a new Trustee, Lewis D. Freeman.

The legal hassles were becoming increasingly complicated and merely served to stymie the effort of local shippers, officials and unions to mount a grass roots campaign to save the railroad. Suggestions were made for sale to assorted interests and for breaking up the railroad into several short lines, but to no avail. Finally the Federal government intervened when railroad retirement taxes were not paid and encouraged the court to liquidate the property. Last-ditch attempts to save the O&W were fruitless and on March 29, 1957, lineside observers turned out to watch the last sad train head for Middletown, dragging a motley collection of equipment bound for sale or scrapping. Through the spring and summer of 1957, the equipment was sold off or cut up and small pieces of track were farmed out to other roads for operation. In August, scrap trains began the sad task of pulling up the rails.

And so it was over. For some the shock was great that such a large railroad could simply be abandoned and torn up, yet most of these people would live to see the debacle of Penn Central and the disappearance of six other venerable names into the colossus called Conrail. In a way and despite its uniqueness, perhaps the O&W was a harbinger of things to come. Too many of us chose to dwell on that uniqueness rather than on the similarities it shared with so many of its Northeastern kin. For now, let us ignore the legal entanglements, the rancor and difficulties and enjoy instead the engines, the trains, all the facets of the best of the O&W in The Final Years. ⊂

-1 class Ten-Wheeler 35 is working up near the freight house as she is recorded on film, perhaor the last time. The 1904 Cooke product was delivered as a 2-6-0, but was rebuilt as a 4-6
n 1919. Note the Ontario Restaurant in the background.

| No. | Builder | Type | Date | Name | Notes |
|---|---|---|---|---|---|
| 86 | Rhode Is. #532 | 4-4-0 | 6/1873 | *Scipio* | Returned to R. I. Wks. 1874. To NJM #81 – NYS&W #11 |
| 87 | Rhode Is. #533 | 4-4-0 | 6/1873 | *Campgaw* | Returned to R. I. Wks. 1874. To NJM #82 – NYS&W #12 |
| 88 | Rhode Is. #534 | 4-4-0 | 6/1873 | *Stockholm* | Returned to R. I. Wks. 1874. To NJM #83 – NYS&W #13 |
| 89 | Rhode Is. #535 | 4-4-0 | 6/1873 | *Oakland* | Ordered but not delivered. Sold to Providence & Worcester RR #30; later NYP&B #130 – NYNH&H #388, then #1745 |
| 90 | Rhode Is. #536 | 4-4-0 | 6/1873 | *Wanaque* | Returned to R. I. Wks. 1874. To NJM #84 – NYS&W #14 |

48 – 18x26 – 74000    Class K

| No. | Builder | Type | Date | Name | Notes |
|---|---|---|---|---|---|
| 91 | Rhode Is. #537 | 2-6-0 | 7/1873 | *Watchung* | Renumb. 102, 1888 |
| 92 | Rhode Is. #538 | 2-6-0 | 7/1873 | *Bloomfield* | Renumb. 103, 1888 |
| 93 | Rhode Is. #539 | 2-6-0 | 7/1873 | *Kearney* | Sold 12/20/1905 |
| 94 | Rhode Is. #540 | 2-6-0 | 7/1873 | *Newark* | Scrapped 10/1908 |
| 95 | Rhode Is. #541 | 2-6-0 | 7/1873 | *Mountain View* | Sold to Sou. Iron & Equip. Co. #1210 8/1917. Resold to Limestone Mfg. Co. #1, 4/1918 |
| 96 | Rhode Is. #542 | 2-6-0 | 7/1873 | *Belleville* | Scrapped 6/22/1910 |
| 97 | Rhode Is. #543 | 2-6-0 | 7/1873 | *Cliffsdale* | Scrapped in 1893 |
| 98 | Rhode Is. #544 | 2-6-0 | 7/1873 | *Ridgewood* | Scrapped 2/1909 |
| 99 | Rhode Is. #545 | 2-6-0 | 8/1873 | *Riverdale* | Scrapped 9/8/1909 |
| 100 | Rhode Is. #546 | 2-6-0 | 8/1873 | *Truxton* | Scrapped in 1896 |
| 101 | Rhode Is. #547 | 2-6-0 | 8/1873 | *Cuyler* | Sold 6/12/1911 |
| 102 | Rhode Is. #537 | 2-6-0 | 7/1873 | *Not named* | Ex 91. Scrapped in 1894 |
| 103 | Rhode Is. #538 | 2-6-0 | 7/1873 | *Not named* | Ex 92. Scrapped 8/11/1905 |

This ends the list of New York & Oswego Midland engines. All subsequent engines were purchased under the new corporate name of New York, Ontario & Western, and were not named. Names were apparently abandoned about 1878.

*Karl E. Schlachter*

In a classic locomotive pose, #72 gives the photographer a broadside turntable view.

Class A. *No. 21* suns herself at Norwich in 1915.

*Karl E. Schlachter*

When *#33* was delivered by Baldwin, the name on the tender suggested what might have been if the New Jersey Midland and Oswego Midland had completed their merger.

Class K. *No. 99* was one of the last engines purchased by the Midland.

# THE STEAM LOCOMOTIVES OF THE NEW YORK, ONTARIO & WESTERN RAILWAY (Continued)

Locomotives purchased or renumbered after change of name in 1880

| No. | BUILDER, BUILDER'S NO. | DATE | DISPOSITION |
|---|---|---|---|
| | Mother Hubbard 4-4-0 | | 68 – 17x24 – 118000 – 80000 – 180   Class B |
| 1 | Cooke #2325 | 11/1895 | First Mother Hubbard 4-4-0. Scrapped 6/10/1916 |
| 2 | Cooke #2339 | 6/1896 | Scrapped 4/1923 |
| | Mother Hubbard 4-4-0 | | 68 – 17x24 – 114000 – 76000 – 180   Class B |
| 3 | Cooke | 7/3/1898 | Rebuilt from 3rd #78. Scrapped 4/1923 |
| 4 | Norwich Shops | 6/20/1898 | Rebuilt from 2nd #76. Scrapped 4/1923 |
| | Single Cab   4-4-0 | | 62 – 17x24 – 87000 – 54000   Class F |
| 7 | Baldwin #2358 | 2/1871 | Ex PJM&NY. 7-PJM&S. 7-Alleghany Valley RR 42. Acq. 1905. Sold 1/1916 |
| | Mother Hubbard   4-4-0 | | 62 – 17x24 – 99000 – 65000 – 180   Class C |
| 10 | Cooke | 1896 | Rebuilt from #36. In service 8/5/96. Scrapped 6/10/1915 |
| 11 | Cooke | 1896 | Rebuilt from #32. In service 12/1/96. Sold for scrap 10/13/1911 |
| 12 | Dickson | 1897 | Rebuilt from #38, orig. #56. In service 3/1897. Scrapped 9/3/1916 |
| 13 | Cooke | 1897 | Rebuilt from #30. In service 10/1897. Sold for scrap 11/1917 |
| 14 | Cooke | 1897 | Rebuilt from #37. In service 10/1897. Scrapped 7/9/1911 |
| 15 | Cooke | 1897 | Rebuilt from #40. In service 10/1897. Scrapped 6/1/1917 |
| 16 | Cooke | 1898 | Rebuilt from #29. In service 6/22/1898. Scrapped 6/8/1911 |
| | Single cab   4-4-0 | | 68 – 18x28 – 135000 – 91000 – 200 – 20100   Class A |
| 20 | Cooke #2476 | 6/1899 | Scrapped 12/31/1932 |
| 21 | Cooke #2494 | 12/1899 | Scrapped 12/31/1932 |
| | Single cab   4-4-0 | | 68 – 18x28 – 142000 – 94000 – 200 – 20100   Class A |
| 22 | Cooke #41333 | 3/1907 | Scrapped 12/31/1932 |
| 23 | Cooke #44800 | 1/1908 | Scrapped 12/31/1932 |
| 24 | Cooke #44801 | 1/1908 | Sold to Middletown & Unionville #6. 7/24/1935 |

## Single cab

**2-6-0  63 – 20x26 – 166900 – 143000 – 190 – 29400  Class I**
**As rebuilt  4-6-0  63 – 20x26 – 192000 – 154000 – 190 – 29400  Class I-1**

| No. | Builder | Date | Notes |
|---|---|---|---|
| 30 | Cooke #28586 | 12/1903 | Rebuilt 5/1921 to 4-6-0. Scrapped 12/31/1940 |
| 31 | Cooke #28587 | 12/1903 | Rebuilt 2/1919 to 4-6-0. Scrapped 12/31/1940 |
| 32 | Cooke #28588 | 12/1903 | Rebuilt 5/1919 to 4-6-0. Scrapped 1/1940 |
| 33 | Cooke #28589 | 12/1903 | Rebuilt 1/1921 to 4-6-0. Sold for scrap 5/21/1948 Luria Bros. |
| 34 | Cooke #28590 | 12/1903 | Rebuilt 6/1920 to 4-6-0. Scrapped 1/1940 |
| 35 | Cooke #28591 | 1/1904 | Rebuilt 11/1919 to 4-6-0. Sold for scrap 7/22/1948 Luria Bros. |
| 36 | Cooke #28592 | 1/1904 | Scrapped 3/1937 |
| 37 | Cooke #28593 | 1/1904 | Scrapped 2/1937 |
| 38 | Cooke #28594 | 1/1904 | Scrapped 3/16/1937 |
| 39 | Cooke #28595 | 1/1904 | Scrapped 2/1937 |

## Single cab

**2-6-0  63 – 20x26 – 170000 – 149000 – 190 – 29400  Class I**

| No. | Builder | Date | Notes |
|---|---|---|---|
| 40 | Baldwin #30636 | 4/1907 | Scrapped 3/1937 |
| 41 | Baldwin #30637 | 4/1907 | Scrapped 3/1937 |
| 42 | Baldwin #30638 | 4/1907 | Sold to Unadilla Valley RR #7 1/4/1945. Scrapped 4/1956 |
| 43 | Baldwin #30673 | 4/1907 | Scrapped 3/1937 |
| 44 | Baldwin #30674 | 4/1907 | Scrapped 3/1937 |

## Mother Hubbard  0-6-0  51 – 20x26 – 156000 – 180 – 32700  Class L

| No. | Builder | Date | Notes |
|---|---|---|---|
| 50 | Cooke #47071 | 4/1910 | Sold for scrap 6/30/45. Mach. Tool & Eq. Corp. Scrapped at Mtwn. 2/47 |
| 51 | Cooke #47072 | 4/1910 | Sold for scrap 6/30/45. Mach. Tool & Eq. Corp. Scrapped at Mtwn. 2/47 |
| 52 | Cooke #47073 | 4/1910 | Sold for scrap 6/30/45. Mach. Tool & Eq. Corp. Scrapped at Mtwn. 2/47 |
| 53 | Cooke #49710 | 5/1911 | Sold for scrap 7/22/1948 Luria Bros. Last 0-6-0 on road |
| 54 | Cooke #49711 | 5/1911 | Sold for scrap 6/30/45. Mach. Tool & Eq. Corp. Scrapped at Mtwn. 2/47 |
| 55 | Brooks #50184 | 5/1911 | Sold for scrap 6/30/45. Mach. Tool & Eq. Corp. Scrapped at Mtwn. 2/47 |
| 56 | Brooks #50185 | 6/1911 | Sold for scrap 6/30/45. Mach. Tool & Eq. Corp. Scrapped at Mtwn. 2/47 |

## Single cab  4-4-0  69 – 18x24 – 116000 – 80000 – 180 – 17200  Class H

| No. | Builder | Date | Notes |
|---|---|---|---|
| 66 | New York #534 | 8/1889 | Retired 10/1932 |
| 67 | New York #535 | 8/1889 | Retired 10/1932 |
| 68 | New York #456 | 3/1889 | Retired 10/1932 |
| 69 | New York #457 | 3/1889 | Retired 10/1932 |

*Jim Shaughnessy*

Class L. Seven chunky switchers like *#55* handled much of O&W yard work.

Class J. This is the old *Dundee*, *#47*, then *#53*, and finally converted to a double-cab job in 1898 as *#115*.

*Harold M. Whiting*

Class A. Revitalized with repairs and paint job, old *24* went to the Middletown and Unionville for a new life.

Class I-1. Originally a 2-6-0 like her sisters, *33* was rebuilt as a ten-wheeler.

## THE STEAM LOCOMOTIVES OF THE NEW YORK, ONTARIO & WESTERN RAILWAY (*Continued*)

| No. | BUILDER, BUILDER's No. | DATE | DISPOSITION |
|---|---|---|---|
| | Single cab | 4-4-0 | 69 – 18x24 – 118000 – 82000 – 180 – 17100   Class G |
| 70 | Brooks #1120 | 6/1886 | Rebuilt Dickson 7/1893. Blew up at Luzon 1907. Scrapped 1907 |
| 71 | Brooks #1121 | 6/1886 | Rebuilt Rome Mach. Works 8/1902. Scrapped 10/1932 |
| 72 | Brooks #1122 | 6/1886 | Rebuilt Dickson 8/1895. Scrapped 12/31/1932 |
| 73 | Brooks #1129 | 7/1886 | Rebuilt Rome Mach. Works 1903. Scrapped 10/31/1932 |
| 74 | Brooks #1130 | 7/1886 | Rebuilt Rome Mach. Works 1905. Scrapped 10/30/1916 |
| 75 | Brooks #1178 | 1/1887 | Rebuilt Rome Mach. Works 1904. Scrapped 10/31/1932 |
| 76 | Brooks #1179 | 1/1887 | Rebuilt to 2nd #4 at Norwich 6/20/1898 |
| 77 | Brooks #1190 | 2/1887 | Rebuilt Rome Mach. Works 11/1903. Scrapped 10/31/1932 |
| 78 | Brooks #1191 | 3/1887 | Rebuilt to 2nd #3 at Cooke 7/3/1898 |
| | Single cab | 2-8-0 | 50 – 20x24 – 115000 – 102000 – 140 – 22800   Class O |
| 80 | Baldwin #7044 | 11/1883 | Ex West Shore 126. Acquired 10/1/1887. Sold to SI&E Co. 10/1917 |
| 81 | Baldwin #7022 | 11/1883 | Ex West Shore 131. Acquired 10/1/1887. Scrapped 10/31/1932 |
| 82 | Baldwin #7074 | 12/1883 | Ex West Shore 132. Acquired 10/1/1887. Scrapped 10/31/1932 |
| 83 | Baldwin #7091 | 12/1883 | Ex West Shore 135. Acquired 5/1886. Sold to SI&E Co. 3/10/20 |
| 84 | Baldwin #7068 | 12/1883 | Ex West Shore 130. Acquired 5/1886. Sold to SI&E Co. 3/30/20 |
| 85 | Baldwin #7131 | 1/1884 | Ex West Shore 143. Acquired 5/1886. Sold to SI&E Co. 3/10/20 |
| 86 | Baldwin #7115 | 1/1884 | Ex West Shore 140. Acquired 5/1886. Sold to SI&E Co. 11/1917 |
| 87 | Baldwin #7036 | 11/1883 | Ex West Shore 125. Acquired 5/1886. Sold to SI&E Co. 10/1917 |
| 88 | Baldwin #7031 | 11/1883 | Ex West Shore 124. Acquired 5/1886. Sold to SI&E Co. 12/1917 |
| 89 | Baldwin #7155 | 2/1884 | Ex West Shore 144. Acquired 10/1/1887. Sold to SI&E Co. 3/20/20 |

Note: #83 sold by SI&E Co. to National of Mexico #13-A 4/17/1920
#84 sold by SI&E Co. to Pittsburgh, Lisbon & Western RR 8/21/1920
#85 sold by SI&E Co. to Greenville & Northern RR 1920
#86 sold by SI&E Co. to Cuba Sugar Cane Corp. #201 1917
#87 sold by SI&E Co. to West Lumber Co. #5, Houston Tex. 1917
#88 sold by SI&E Co. to Cuba Sugar Cane Corp. #202 1917
#89 apparently scrapped by SI&E Co.

**Single cab  2-8-0  50 – 20x24 – 100000 – 130 – 21200**

| No. | Builder | Date | Notes |
|---|---|---|---|
| 90 | Dickson #228 | 3/1879 | Orig, Boston, Hoosac Tunnel & Western #5. Sold to Sinnemahoning Valley #2. Acquired 5/16/1887. Rebuilt to #189 5/1899 |

**Single cab  2-8-0  50 – 20x24 – 119000 – 105000 – 150 – 24500   Class N**

| No. | Builder | Date | Notes |
|---|---|---|---|
| 91 | New York #323 | 1/1888 | Sold for scrap 1/22/1929 |
| 92 | New York #324 | 1/1888 | Sold for scrap 1/22/1929 |

**Single cab  2-6-0  62 – 19x24 – 128000 – 112000 – 175 – 20800   Class M**

| No. | Builder | Date | Notes |
|---|---|---|---|
| 104 | New York #458 | 3/1889 | Sold to Unadilla Valley RR #3 10/22/1915 |
| 105 | New York #459 | 3/1889 | Sold for scrap 1/22/1929 |
| 106 | New York #562 | 11/1889 | Sold for scrap 1/22/1929 |
| 107 | New York #563 | 11/1889 | Sold for scrap 1/22/1929 |
| 108 | New York #564 | 12/1889 | Sold for scrap 10/31/1932 |
| 109 | New York #565 | 2/1890 | Sold to SI&E Co. 7/1913 |
| 110 | New York #566 | 2/1890 | Scrapped 3/1929 |
| 111 | New York #567 | 2/1890 | Scrapped 10/31/1935 |

#109 sold by SI&E Co. to J. M. Griffin #2, Nomac, Miss. 8/26/1913. Returned 11/1913. Resold to Central Santo Domingo #2, Cuba, 1914

**Mother Hubbard  2-6-0  57 – 17x24 – 99000 – 84000   Class J**

| No. | Builder | Date | Notes |
|---|---|---|---|
| 115 | Cooke | 12/1898 | Rebuilt from 2nd 53, orig. 1st 47. Scrapped 12/30/1915 |
| 116 | Cooke | 12/1898 | Rebuilt from 63. Scrapped 6/1917 |
| 117 | Rome Mach. Works | 1902 | Rebuilt from 59. Scrapped 10/27/1913 |
| 118 | Rome Mach. Works | 1902 | Rebuilt from 2nd 55, orig. 1st 43. Scrapped 10/7/1915 |
| 119 | Rome Mach. Works | 1902 | Rebuilt from 61. Scrapped 6/1908 |
| 120 | Rome Mach. Works | 1902 | Rebuilt from 62. Scrapped 6/1917 |
| 121 | Rome Mach. Works | 1902 | Rebuilt from 64. Scrapped 11/17/1913 |

**Mother Hubbard  2-6-0  56 – 19x24 – 118000 – 103000   Class R**

| No. | Builder | Date | Notes |
|---|---|---|---|
| 126 | Dickson #763 | 6/1890 | Sold for scrap 2/28/1923 |
| 127 | Dickson #764 | 6/1890 | Sold for scrap 11/1917 |
| 128 | Dickson #765 | 6/1890 | Sold for scrap 11/1917 |

*John Stellwagen*

Class S. This Dickson hog acquired the only known Vanderbilt tender on the railroad.

Class U. These engines were popular passenger haulers and here *#255* stands at Monticello with a camp special.

*Jack Farrell*

Class G. Second *71* was a trim and graceful beauty, seen here at Walton.

Class I. This Mogul went to the Unadilla Valley as their *No. 7.*

# THE STEAM LOCOMOTIVES OF THE NEW YORK, ONTARIO & WESTERN RAILWAY (*Continued*)

| No. | BUILDER, BUILDER'S No. | DATE | DISPOSITION |
|---|---|---|---|
| 129 | Dickson #766 | 6/1890 | Sold for scrap 2/27/1918 |
| 130 | Dickson #767 | 7/1890 | Scrapped 1/22/1929 |
| 131 | Dickson #768 | 7/1890 | Blew up in 1909. New boiler 12/10/09. Scrapped 2/6/1935 |
| 132 | Dickson #769 | 7/1890 | Scrapped 1/22/1929 |
| 133 | Dickson #770 | 7/1890 | Sold for scrap 4/1923 |
| 134 | Dickson #771 | 7/1890 | Sold for scrap 2/21/1923 |
| 135 | Dickson #772 | 8/1890 | Scrapped 10/1925 |
| 136 | Dickson #709 | 7/1889 | Blt. as NYO&W #111. Renmb. #211 2/1890. Renmb. #136 8/1890. Scr. 5/1917 |

Single cab 2-6-0 56 – 18x24 – 112000 – 98000 Class Q

| No. | BUILDER, BUILDER'S No. | DATE | DISPOSITION |
|---|---|---|---|
| 137 | Dickson #819 | 6/1892 | Sold to SI&E Co. 12/20/1915. Resold to Brown Lbr. Co. #137, Hiwanee, Miss. 1/16/1916 |
| 138 | Dickson #820 | 6/1892 | Sold to SI&E Co. 3/4/1916. Resold to Carolina & Yadkin River #105, High Point, N.C. 4/12/1916 |

Mother Hubbard 2-6-0 62 – 19x24 – 135000 – 119000 – 180 – 21400 Class T

| No. | BUILDER, BUILDER'S No. | DATE | DISPOSITION |
|---|---|---|---|
| 139 | Dickson #897 | 1/1893 | Sold for scrap 2/6/1935 |
| 140 | Dickson #904 | 4/1893 | Sold for scrap 2/6/1935 |
| 141 | Dickson #905 | 4/1893 | Sold for scrap 2/6/1935 |
| 142 | Dickson #906 | 4/1893 | Sold for scrap 2/6/1935 |
| 143-144 – See 248-249 | | | |
| 146-147 – See 246-247 | | | |

Mother Hubbard 2-8-0 50 – 20x24 – 136000 – 119000 – 160 – 26100 Class S

| No. | BUILDER, BUILDER'S No. | DATE | DISPOSITION |
|---|---|---|---|
| 151 | Dickson #773 | 8/1890 | Scrapped 8/31/1918 |
| 152 | Dickson #774 | 8/1890 | Scrapped 10/1914 |
| 153 | Dickson #775 | 8/1890 | Sold for scrap 10/1925 |
| 154 | Dickson #776 | 9/1890 | Scrapped 10/1925 |
| 155 | Dickson #777 | 9/1890 | Sold for scrap 10/1925 |

| 156 | Dickson #778 | 10/1890 | Scrapped 3/1924 |
| 157 | Dickson #779 | 10/1890 | Scrapped 5/18/1937. Last Dickson engine on the road |
| 158 | Dickson #780 | 10/1890 | Sold for scrap 1/22/1929 |
| 159 | Dickson #781 | 10/1890 | Sold for scrap 1/22/1929 |
| 160 | Dickson #782 | 10/1890 | Scrapped 6/1916 |
| 161 | Dickson #783 | 10/1890 | Retired 10/31/1932. Scrapped in 1933 |
| 162 | Dickson #784 | 12/1890 | Scrapped 7/31/1933 |
| 163 | Dickson #785 | 12/1890 | Sold for scrap 1/22/1929 |
| 164 | Dickson #786 | 12/1890 | Sold for scrap 4/1923 |
| 165 | Dickson #787 | 12/1890 | Retired 10/31/1932. Scrapped 1935 |
| 166 | Dickson #873 | 7/1892 | Retired 10/31/1932. Scrapped 1935 |
| 167 | Dickson #874 | 7/1892 | Sold for scrap 3/1923 |
| 168 | Dickson #875 | 7/1892 | Scrapped 1/28/1913 |
| 169 | Dickson #876 | 7/1892 | Scrapped 4/1923 |
| 170 | Dickson #877 | 7/1892 | Scrapped 9/30/1918 |
| 171 | Dickson #878 | 8/1892 | Sold for scrap 10/1925 |
| 172 | Dickson #879 | 8/1892 | Sold for scrap 4/1923 |
| 173 | Dickson #880 | 8/1892 | Sold for scrap 10/1925 |
| 174 | Dickson #881 | 8/1892 | Retired 10/31/1932. Scrapped 1935 |
| 175 | Dickson #882 | 8/1892 | Scrapped 8/1925 |
| 176 | Dickson #883 | 9/1892 | Scrapped 1/19/1925 |
| 177 | Dickson #884 | 9/1892 | Retired 10/31/1932. Scrapped 1935 |
| 178 | Dickson #885 | 10/1892 | Retired 10/31/1932. Scrapped 1935 |
| 179 | Dickson #886 | 10/1892 | Retired 10/31/1932. Scrapped 1935 |
| 180 | Dickson #887 | 10/1892 | Sold for scrap 3/1923 |
| 181 | Dickson #898 | 3/1893 | Blew up 7/1895. Reblt Cooke 1/1896, new boiler. Retired 10/31/32. Scr. 1935 |
| 182 | Dickson #899 | 3/1893 | Retired 10/31/1932. Scrapped 1935 |
| 183 | Dickson #900 | 3/1893 | Retired 10/31/1932. Scrapped 1935 |
| 184 | Dickson #901 | 3/1893 | Sold for scrap 10/1925 |
| 185 | Dickson #902 | 3/1893 | Scrapped 7/31/1933 |
| 186 | Dickson #903 | 4/1893 | Retired 10/31/1932. Scrapped 1935 |
| 187 | Dickson #907 | 6/1894 | Retired 10/31/1932. Scrapped 1935. (Blt. 5/1893 – held at factory 14 mos.) |

Class W-2. With air pumps moved forward, *No. 302* presented a contrast to the appearance of
Class W companions.

*Stephen D. Maguire*

Class E. Caught in a Northern Division snowstorm, *#225* makes a nostalgic picture.

Class P. *No. 218* was a consolidation in the center-cab tradition.

*Stephen D. Maguire*

## THE STEAM LOCOMOTIVES OF THE NEW YORK, ONTARIO & WESTERN RAILWAY (Continued)

| No. | Builder, Builder's No. | Date | Disposition |
|---|---|---|---|
| 188 | Dickson #908 | 6/1894 | Scrapped 3/1929 (Blt. 5/1893 – held at factory 14 mos.) |
| 189 | Dickson #228 | 3/1879 | Ex NYO&W 2nd 90 – 2nd 89 – SV 2 – BHT&W 5. Reblt. Cooke 5/1899. Scrapped 1/28/18 |
| 190 | Rome Mach. Works | 1907 | Rebuilt. Acq. 5/22/07 from Erie RR, Class H-4, road number unknown, chassis only. New boiler installed as Mother Hubbard at Rome Mach. Works. Retired 10/31/1932. Scr. 1934. |
| 191 | Dickson #911 | 12/1893 | Held at factory until 11/18/1895. Retired 10/31/32. Scrapped 1935. |
| 192 | Dickson #912 | 12/1893 | Held at factory until 11/18/1895. Sold for scrap 4/1923 |

Class P   Mother Hubbard   2-8-0   55 – 21x32 – 200000 – 178000 – 200 – 44300

| No. | Builder, Builder's No. | Date | Disposition |
|---|---|---|---|
| 201 | Cooke #2509 | 2/1900 | Sold to Luria Bros. 2/11/47. Scrapped at Mtwn. 4/1947 |
| 202 | Cooke #2566 | 8/1900 | Sold to Luria Bros. 2/11/47. Scrapped at Mtwn. 4/1947 |
| 203 | Cooke #2567 | 8/1900 | Sold to Luria Bros. 2/20/48. Shipped off line. |
| 204 | Cooke #2568 | 8/1900 | Scrapped prior 1947 |
| 205 | Cooke #2646 | 3/1901 | Sold to Luria Bros. 2/11/47. Scrapped at Mtwn. 4/1947 |
| 206 | Cooke #2647 | 3/1901 | Scrapped 12/24/1936 |
| 207 | Cooke #2648 | 3/1901 | Sold to Luria Bros. 4/13/48. Shipped off line |
| 208 | Cooke #2649 | 3/1901 | Sold to Luria Bros. 6/29/48. Shipped off line |
| 209 | Cooke #2650 | 3/1901 | Scrapped prior 1947 |
| 210 | Cooke #2651 | 3/1901 | Scrapped 8/7/1947 |
| 211 | Cooke #2710 | 9/1901 | Scrapped prior 1947 |
| 212 | Cooke #2711 | 9/1901 | Scrapped 4/1937 |
| 213 | Cooke #2712 | 9/1901 | Sold to Luria Bros. 7/13/48. Shipped off line |
| 214 | Cooke #2713 | 9/1901 | Scrapped prior 1947 |
| 215 | Cooke #26242 | 6/1902 | Scrapped prior 1947 |
| 216 | Cooke #26243 | 6/1902 | Sold to Luria Bros. 5/11/48. Shipped off line |
| 217 | Cooke #26244 | 6/1902 | Scrapped 8/17/47 |
| 218 | Cooke #29286 | 3/1904 | Sold to Luria Bros. 2/20/48. Shipped off line |
| 219 | Cooke #29287 | 3/1904 | Scrapped 1947 |
| 220 | Cooke #29288 | 3/1904 | Sold to Luria Bros. 2/22/48. Shipped off line |

Class E Single cab 4-6-0 69 – 21x26 – 180000 – 134000 – 195 – 27200

| 225 | Brooks #50035 | 5/1911 | Sold to Luria Bros. 2/11/47. Scrapped 4/1947 at Mtwn. |
| 226 | Brooks #50036 | 5/1911 | Sold to Luria Bros. 4/29/48. Shipped off line |
| 227 | Brooks #50037 | 5/1911 | Sold to Luria Bros. 5/19/48. Shipped off line |
| 228 | Brooks #50038 | 5/1911 | Sold to Luria Bros. 2/11/47. Scrapped 4/1947 at Mtwn. |

Classes U and U-1 Mother Hubbard 2-6-0 as built.

Dimensions as 2-6-0s: 69 – 20x28 – 161000 – 138000 – 190 – 28900    Class U
Dimensions as 4-6-0s: 69 – 21x28 – 184000 – 141000 – 200 – 30400    Class U-1

| 240 | Cooke #30446 | 2/1905 | Class U; not rebuilt. Scrapped 3/1937 |
| 241 | Cooke #30447 | 2/1905 | Class U-1, rebuilt 8/20. Scrapped 5/18/1937 |
| 242 | Cooke #30448 | 2/1905 | Class U; not rebuilt. Scrapped 1/1940 |
| 243 | Cooke #29283 | 5/1904 | Class U; not rebuilt. Scrapped 3/1937 |
| 244 | Cooke #29284 | 5/1904 | Class U-1, rebuilt 7/1917. Sold to Luria Bros. 3/5/48. Shipped off line |
| 245 | Cooke #29285 | 5/1904 | Class U-1, reblt. 12/24. Sold to Luria Bros. 2/11/47. Scr. 4/1947 at Mtwn. |
| 246 | Cooke #27493 | 3/1903 | Class U-1, reblt. 7/17. Sold to Summer & Co. 3/29/46. Scr. 2/1947 at Mtwn. |
| 247 | Cooke #27493 | 3/1903 | Class U; not rebuilt. Scrapped 2/1937 |
| 248 | Cooke #2645 | 6/1901 | Class U; not rebuilt. Scrapped 2/6/1935 |
| 249 | Dickson #1218 | 7/1901 | Class U-1, rebuilt 6/17. Scrapped 10/24/1936 |
| 250 | Cooke #30449 | 2/1905 | Class U-1, rebuilt 10/19. Retired 12/1940. Scrapped 6/1942 |
| 251 | Cooke #38971 | 11/1905 | Class U-1, rebuilt 12/16. Retired 12/1940. Scrapped 6/1942 |
| 252 | Cooke #38972 | 11/1905 | Class U, not rebuilt. Scrapped 3/1937 |
| 253 | Cooke #38973 | 11/1905 | Class U-1, rebuilt 3/23. Retired 12/1940. Scrapped 6/1942 |
| 254 | Cooke #38974 | 11/1905 | Class U; not rebuilt. Scrapped 7/1942 |
| 255 | Cooke #38975 | 11/1905 | Class U; not rebuilt. Sold to Mach. Tool & Eq. Co. 6/30/46. Scrapped 2/47 |
| 256 | Cooke #38976 | 11/1905 | Class U-1, rebuilt 9/17. Retired 12/1940; scrapped 6/1942 |

Note: Engine 243 was purchased as 143. Engine 248 was purchased as 143. Wrecked in head-on collision with 144 and rebuilt. Renumbered 148, 5/1903. Renumbered 248, 2/1905.
Engine 244 was purchased as 144. Engine 249 was purchased as 144. Wrecked as above. Reblt. and renum. 149, 5/1903. Renumbered 249, 2/1905.
Engine 245 was purchased as 145.
Engine 246 was purchased as 146. Renumbered 2/1905.
Engine 247 was purchased as 147. Renumbered 2/1905.

*Jack Farrell*

Class Y. *No. 405* is shown here before stylist Otto Kuhler gave her the modernization treatment.

Class Y-2. One of the heavy Mountains has her standard winter equipment — a butterfly plow.

*Jack Farrell*

Class **X**. A Bullmoose rests at Middletown.

Class **Y**. A builder's photo shows why the *Light 400's* pleased the eye.

# THE STEAM LOCOMOTIVES OF THE NEW YORK, ONTARIO & WESTERN RAILWAY (Continued)

| No. | Builder, Builder's No. | Date | Disposition |
|---|---|---|---|
| | **Class V   Mother Hubbard   2-6-0  63 – 20x28 – 174000 – 150000 – 200 – 31600** | | |
| 271 | Cooke #45420 | 6/1908 | Sold to Mach. Tool & Eq. Co. 6/30/46. Scrapped 2/1947 |
| 272 | Cooke #45421 | 6/1908 | Sold to Unadilla Valley RR 8/1941 |
| 273 | Cooke #45422 | 6/1908 | Sold to Mach. Tool & Eq. Co. 6/30/46. Scrapped 2/1947 |
| 274 | Cooke #45423 | 6/1908 | Retired 12/1940. Scrapped 6/1942 |
| 275 | Cooke #45660 | 10/1908 | Retired 12/1940. Scrapped 6/1942 |
| 276 | Cooke #45661 | 10/1908 | Scrapped 1/1940 |
| 277 | Cooke #45662 | 10/1908 | Sold to Mach. Tool & Eq. Co. 6/30/46. Scrapped 2/1947 |
| 278 | Cooke #45663 | 10/1908 | Sold to Mach. Tool & Eq. Co. 6/30/46. Scrapped 2/1947 |
| 279 | Cooke #45664 | 10/1908 | Retired 12/1940. Scrapped 6/1942 |
| 280 | Cooke #45665 | 10/1908 | Retired 12/1940. Scrapped 6/1942 |
| 281 | Cooke #45841 | 1/1909 | Retired 12/1940. Sold to UV, then traded for #42, scrapped by O&W |
| 282 | Cooke #45842 | 1/1909 | Scrapped 1/1940 |
| 283 | Cooke #45843 | 1/1909 | Scrapped 12/13/1938 |
| 284 | Cooke #45844 | 1/1909 | Sold to Mach. Tool & Eq. Co. 6/30/46. Scrapped 2/1947 |
| 285 | Cooke #45424 | 6/1908 | Blt. as Scranton Coal Co. #100. Acq. 2/1/09 as NYO&W #100; renumb. 285, 2/17/1909. Scrapped 1/1940 |
| | **Class W and W-2   Single cab   2-8-0  55 – 21x32 – 206000 – 182000 – 200 – 45400** | | |
| 301 | Cooke #48137 | 7/1910 | W. Sold to Luria Bros. 2/20/48. |
| 302 | Cooke #48138 | 7/1910 | W-2. Sold to Luria Bros. 7/16/48 |
| 303 | Cooke #48139 | 7/1910 | W-2. Sold to Luria Bros. 2/20/48 |
| 304 | Cooke #48140 | 7/1910 | W-2. Sold to Luria Bros. 7/20/48 |
| 305 | Cooke #48141 | 7/1910 | W-2. Sold to Luria Bros. 4/8/48 |
| 306 | Cooke #48142 | 7/1910 | W-2. Sold to Luria Bros. 4/8/48 |
| 307 | Cooke #48355 | 7/1910 | W-2. Sold to Luria Bros. 4/14/48 |
| 308 | Cooke #48356 | 7/1910 | W-2. Sold to Luria Bros. 7/8/48 |
| 309 | Cooke #48357 | 7/1910 | W. Sold to Luria Bros. 6/21/48 |

| No. | Builder | Date | Notes |
| --- | --- | --- | --- |
| 310 | Cooke #48358 | 7/1910 | W-2. Sold to Luria Bros. 2/11/47 |
| 311 | Cooke #48359 | 7/1910 | W-2. Sold to Luria Bros. 7/22/48 |
| 312 | Cooke #48360 | 7/1910 | W. Sold to Mach. Tool & Eq. Co. 6/30/48 |
| 313 | Cooke #48362 | 7/1910 | W. Sold to Luria Bros. 7/19/48 |
| 314 | Cooke #48363 | 7/1910 | W. Sold to Luria Bros. 7/16/48 |
| 315 | Cooke #49410 | 2/1911 | W-2. Sold to Luria Bros. 7/16/48 |
| 316 | Cooke #49411 | 2/1911 | W. Sold to Luria Bros. 7/16/48 |
| 317 | Cooke #49412 | 2/1911 | W. Sold to Luria Bros. 7/13/48 |
| 318 | Cooke #49413 | 2/1911 | W. Sold to Luria Bros. 2/11/47 |
| 319 | Cooke #49414 | 2/1911 | W. Sold to Luria Bros. 7/13/48 |
| 320 | Cooke #49415 | 2/1911 | W. Sold to Luria Bros. 7/22/48 |
| 321 | Cooke #49704 | 3/1911 | W. Sold to Luria Bros. 7/22/48 |
| 322 | Cooke #49705 | 3/1911 | W. Sold to Luria Bros. 5/8/48 |
| 323 | Cooke #49706 | 3/1911 | W. Sold to Luria Bros. 7/22/48 |
| 324 | Cooke #49707 | 3/1911 | W. Sold to Luria Bros. 5/17/48 |
| 325 | Cooke #49708 | 3/1911 | W. Sold to Mach. Tool & Equip. Co. 6/30/46 |
| 326 | Cooke #49709 | 3/1911 | W. Sold to Mach. Tool & Equip. Co. 6/30/46 |

**Class X   Single cab   2-10-2   57 – 28x32 – 352000 – 293000 – 190 – 71200**

| No. | Builder | Date | Notes |
| --- | --- | --- | --- |
| 351 | Schen. #55268 | 10/1915 | Scrapped 6/1946 |
| 352 | Schen. #55269 | 10/1915 | Scrapped 3/1946 |
| 353 | Schen. #55270 | 10/1915 | Sold to Summer & Co. for scrap 7/1943 |
| 354 | Schen. #55271 | 10/1915 | Scrapped 4/1944 |
| 355 | Schen. #55272 | 10/1915 | Retired 12/1940. Scrapped 6/1942. Class X-1 |
| 356 | Schen. #55273 | 10/1915 | Scrapped 6/1946 |
| 357 | Schen. #55274 | 10/1915 | Scrapped 5/31/1940 |
| 358 | Schen. #55275 | 10/1915 | Scrapped 3/1946 |
| 359 | Schen. #55276 | 10/1915 | Sold to Summer & Co. for scrap 7/1943 |
| 360 | Schen. #55277 | 10/1915 | Scrapped 3/1946 |
| 361 | Schen. #55278 | 10/1915 | Scrapped 3/1946 |
| 362 | Schen. #55279 | 10/1915 | Retired 12/1940. Scrapped 6/1942 |

*Robert Larson*

Some of the O&W power went west. Here is O&W *503*, backed by *501-A*, as renumbered and repainted by Western Pacific and Sacramento Northern.

Two EMD road-switchers enjoy a Sunday siesta in Cadosia yard.

*Jim Shaughnessy*

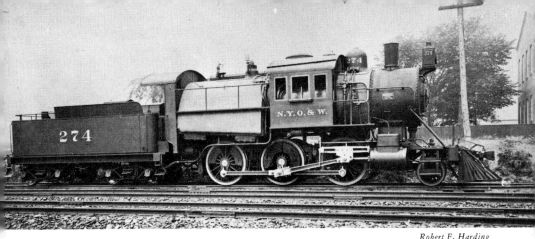

*Robert F. Harding*

Class V. Slower than the U's, these Mother Hubbards were handsome steamers when they were delivered in 1908.

Class W. Rugged and flexible, these locomotives could serve as switchers as well as road engines.

*John Stellwagen*

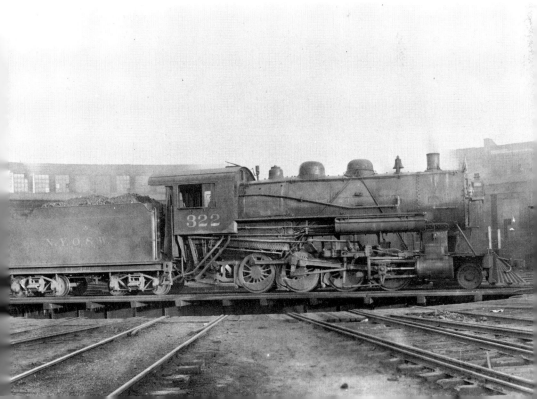

# THE STEAM LOCOMOTIVES OF THE NEW YORK, ONTARIO & WESTERN RAILWAY (Continued)

| No. | Builder, Builder's No. | Date | Disposition |
|---|---|---|---|
| | | | Class Y and Y-1  Single cab  4-8-2  69 — 27x28 — 317000 — 208000 — 200 — 50300 |
| 401 | Schen. #63254 | 5/1922 | Sold to Savannah & Atlanta #445 6/9/1945 |
| 402 | Schen. #63255 | 5/1922 | Y-1. Sold to Luria Bros. 8/28/48. Last steam locomotive on road. |
| 403 | Schen. #63256 | 5/1922 | Sold to Luria Bros. 4/23/48 |
| 404 | Schen. #63257 | 5/1922 | Sold to Savannah & Atlanta #448 6/9/1945 |
| 405 | Schen. #64735 | 10/1923 | Sold to Luria Bros. 4/28/48 |
| 406 | Schen. #64736 | 10/1923 | Sold to Savannah & Atlanta #447 6/9/1945 |
| 407 | Schen. #64737 | 10/1923 | Sold to Savannah & Atlanta #449 6/9/1945 |
| 408 | Schen. #64738 | 10/1923 | Sold to Luria Bros. 4/30/48 |
| 409 | Schen. #64739 | 10/1923 | Sold to Savannah & Atlanta #446 6/9/1945 |
| 410 | Schen. #64740 | 10/1923 | Sold to Luria Bros. 2/11/47. Scrapped at Mtwn. 4/1947 |
| | | | Class Y-2  Single cab  4-8-2  69 — 27x30 — 360000 — 239500 — 225 — 60620 |
| 451 | Schen. #67986 | 7/1929 | Sold to Luria Bros. 3/17/48 |
| 452 | Schen. #67987 | 7/1929 | Sold to Bangor & Aroostook RR #120 6/10/45 |
| 453 | Schen. #67988 | 7/1929 | Sold to Luria Bros. 3/29/48 |
| 454 | Schen. #67989 | 7/1929 | Sold to Bangor & Aroostook RR #121 6/10/45 |
| 455 | Schen. #67990 | 7/1929 | Sold to Bangor & Aroostook RR #124 6/10/45 |
| 456 | Schen. #67991 | 7/1929 | Sold to Luria Bros. 2/11/47. Scrapped at Mtwn. 3/1947 |
| 457 | Schen. #67992 | 7/1929 | Sold to Luria Bros. 2/11/47 |
| 458 | Schen. #67993 | 7/1929 | Sold to Luria Bros. 7/19/48 |
| 459 | Schen. #67994 | 7/1929 | Sold to Bangor & Aroostook RR #122 6/10/45 |
| 460 | Schen. #67995 | 7/1929 | Sold to Bangor & Aroostook RR #123 6/10/45 |
| | | | Mother Hubbard  2-8-0  56 — 21x30 — 195000 — 200 — 42100 |
| 701 | Dickson #27516 | 1/1903 | Ex D&H 2nd 805; previously D&H 844; originally D&H 223. Acquired 8/9/1947. Sold for scrap 6/22/48 |

Locomotives previously listed, but renumbered at various dates listed below

| No. | Type | Previous Nos. | Disposition |
|---|---|---|---|
| 2nd 20 | 0-4-0 | Ex 1st 46 | Renumbered 1/27/1889. Retired by 1893 |
| 2nd 23 | 0-4-0 | Ex 1st 27 | Renumbered 1/22/1889. Sold in 1900 |
| 2nd 25 | 4-4-0 | Ex 3rd 65; ex 2nd 69; ex 1st 82 | Renumbered 7/1/1889. Sold 1/7/1905 |
| 2nd 26 | 4-4-0 | Ex 2nd 66; ex 1st 80 | Renumb. 8/1/1889. Converted to Inspection Eng. 8/1893. Reblt. Mdtwn. 1903. Retired 12/31/1932. Scrapped 1935 |
| 2nd 27 | 4-4-0 | Ex 1st 67; ex 1st 81 | Renumb. 9/19/1889. Sold to Port Jervis, Monticello & New York RR #5 9/1/1899; wrecked 9/18/1899 at Port Jervis; returned to NYO&W as #27; Sold to Shop Dept. 7/1903 |
| 2nd 28 | 4-4-0 | Ex 1st 38 | Renumb. 2/2/1889. Converted to Inspection Engine. Cab transferred to 2nd 26, 8/1893 and engine scrapped |
| 3rd 28 | 4-4-0 | Ex 1st 41 | Renumb. 11/7/1906. Scrapped 7/1909 |
| 2nd 33 | 4-4-0 | Ex 1st 54 | Renumb. 1/26/1889. Scrapped 6/1901 |
| 2nd 38 | 4-4-0 | Ex 1st 56 | Renumb. 2/3/1889. Reblt. to 2nd 12 at Dickson 3/1897 |
| 2nd 43 | 4-4-0 | Ex 1st 55 | Renumbered 1/29/1889. Scrapped 8/16/1905 |
| 2nd 48 | 2-6-0 | Ex 2nd 65; ex 2nd 78; ex 1st 68; ex 1st 79 | Scrapped 1899 |
| 2nd 49 | 2-6-0 | Ex 2nd 68; ex 1st 78 | Rebuilt to 0-6-0. Scrapped 3/1900 |
| 2nd 53 | 2-6-0 | Ex 1st 47 | Rebuilt to #115 12/1898 |
| 2nd 54 | 2-6-0 | Ex 1st 33 | Sold to Sou. Iron & Equip. Co. 7/24/1907. Resold to Martel Lmbr. Co. #238, Martel, Fla. 6/29/1908; later Roux-Denton Lmbr. Co. #238 |
| 2nd 55 | 2-6-0 | Ex 1st 43 | Rebuilt to #118 in 1902 |
| 2nd 56 | 2-6-0 | Ex 1st 45 | Sold for scrap 1907 |
| 2nd 65 | 2-6-0 | Ex 2nd 78; ex 1st 68; ex 1st 79 | Renumbered 2nd 48, 2/16/1889 |
| 3rd 65 | 4-4-0 | Ex 2nd 69; ex 1st 82 | Renumbered 2nd 25 7/1/1889 |
| 1st 66 | 4-4-0 | Ex 1st 80 | Renumbered 2nd 26, 8/1/1889 |
| 1st 67 | 4-4-0 | Ex 1st 81 | Renumbered 2nd 27, 9/19/1889 |
| 2nd 68 | 2-6-0 | Ex 1st 78 | Renumbered 2nd 49, 2/4/1889 |
| 2nd 69 | 4-4-0 | Ex 1st 82 | Renumbered 3rd 65, 2/16/1889 |
| 2nd 78 | 2-6-0 | Ex 1st 68; ex 1st 79 | Renumbered 2nd 65, 1887 |
| 2nd 89 | 2-8-0 | Ex Sinnemahoning Valley #2; BHT&W #5 | Acq. 5/16/87. Renumbered 2nd 90, 10/2/1887 |

# THE DIESEL-ELECTRIC LOCOMOTIVES OF THE NEW YORK, ONTARIO & WESTERN RAILWAY

| No. | Builder/No. | Delivery Date | | | Disposition |
|---|---|---|---|---|---|
| | | **Class D** | **Switcher** | **33 — B-B — 88,000 — 26,400 — 380** | |
| 101 | G.E. #15028 | 12/1941 | | | Sold to Hyman-Michaels 1951, to Salt Lake, Garfield & Western DS-1 |
| 102 | G.E. #15029 | 12/1941 | | | Sold to Mississippi Export RR 6/1950, to Fernwood, Columbia & Gulf, to Fort Dodge, Des Moines & Southern #502 |
| 103 | G.E. #15030 | 12/1941 | | | Sold to Fernwood, Columbia & Gulf 8/1950, to FDD & S #503 |
| 104 | G.E. #15031 | 1/1942 | | | Sold to Frank M. Judge Co. 6/1952, to Great Northern Paper #5 |
| 105 | G.E. #15032 | 8/1942 | | | Sold to Hyman-Michaels 1951, to SLG & W DS-2 |
| | | **Class G** | **Road switcher NW-2** | **40 — B-B — 248,000 — 62,500 — 1,000** | |
| 111 | EMD #3164 | 3/1948 | | | Sold to M.S. Kaplan, to Rock Island #795 |
| 112 | EMD #3165 | 3/1948 | | | Sold to M.S. Kaplan, to Rock Island #796 |
| 113 | EMD #3166 | 3/1948 | | | Sold to M.S. Kaplan, to Rock Island #797 |
| 114 | EMD #3167 | 3/1948 | | | Sold to NYC 6/1957, to NYC 9500, to PC 8683 |
| 115 | EMD #3168 | 4/1948 | | | Sold to Northern Pacific 6/1957, NP #99 |
| 116 | EMD #3169 | 6/1948 | | | Sold to NYC 6/1957, NYC #9501, to PC #8684 |
| 117 | EMD #3170 | 6/1948 | | | Sold to NYC 6/1957, NYC #9502, to PC #8685 |
| 118 | EMD #3171 | 6/1948 | | | Sold to NYC 6/1957, NYC #9503, to PC #8686 |
| 119 | EMD #3172 | 6/1948 | | | Sold to NYC 6/1957, NYC #9504, to PC #8687 |
| 120 | EMD #3173 | 6/1948 | | | Sold to NYC 6/1957, NYC #9505, to PC #8688 |
| 121 | EMD #3174 | 6/1948 | | | Sold to NYC 6/1957, NYC #9506, to PC #8689 |
| 122 | EMD #3175 | 6/1948 | | | Sold to NYC 6/1957, NYC #9507, to PC #8690 |
| 123 | EMD #3176 | 6/1948 | | | Sold to NYC 6/1957, NYC #9508, to PC #8691 |
| 124 | EMD #3177 | 7/1948 | | | Sold to NYC 6/1957, NYC #9509, to PC #8692 |
| 125 | EMD #3178 | 7/1948 | | | Sold to NYC 6/1957, NYC #9510, to PC #8693 |
| 126 | EMD #3179 | 7/1948 | | | Sold to NYC 6/1957, NYC #9511, to PC #8694 |
| 127 | EMD #3180 | 7/1948 | | | Sold to NYC 6/1957, NYC #9512, to PC #8695 |
| 128 | EMD #6160 | 7/1948 | | | Sold to NYC 6/1957, NYC #9513, to PC #8696 |
| 129 | EMD #6161 | 7/1948 | | | Sold to NYC 6/1957, NYC #9514, to PC #8697 |
| 130 | EMD #6162 | 7/1948 | | | Sold to NYC 6/1957, NYC #9515, to PC #8698 |
| 131 | EMD #6163 | 7/1948 | | | Sold to NYC 6/1957, NYC #9516, to PC #8699 |

## Class B — Freight locomotive F3 — 40 — B-B — 232,000 — 57,500 — 1500

| | | | |
|---|---|---|---|
| 501 | EMD #3146 | 1/1948 | Sold to Hyman-Michaels 6/1957, to Sacramento Northern #301 |
| 502 | EMD #3147 | 2/1948 | Sold to Hyman-Michaels 6/1957, to Sacramento Northern #302 |
| 503 | EMD #3148 | 3/1948 | Sold to Hyman-Michaels 6/1957, to Western Pacific #801-D |

## Class A — Freight locomotive FT — 40 — B-B+B-B — 458,000 — 114,500 — 2700

| | | | |
|---|---|---|---|
| 601A | EMD #3139 | 5/1945 | Sold to Harold Gottfried 6/1957 |
| 601B | EMD #3141 | 5/1945 | Sold to Harold Gottfried 6/1957 |
| 801A | EMD #3123 | 5/1945 | Sold to Harold Gottfried 6/1957 |
| 801B | EMD #3131 | 5/1945 | Sold to Harold Gottfried 6/1957 |
| 802A | EMD #3124 | 5/1945 | Sold to Harold Gottfried 6/1957 |
| 802B | EMD #3132 | 5/1945 | Sold to Harold Gottfried 6/1957 |
| 803A | EMD #3125 | 5/1945 | Sold to Harold Gottfried 6/1957 |
| 803B | EMD #3133 | 5/1945 | Sold to Harold Gottfried 6/1957 |
| 804A | EMD #3126 | 5/1945 | Sold to Harold Gottfried 6/1957 |
| 804B | EMD #3134 | 5/1945 | Sold to Harold Gottfried 6/1957 |
| 805A | EMD #3127 | 5/1945 | Sold to Harold Gottfried 6/1957 |
| 805B | EMD #3135 | 5/1945 | Sold to Harold Gottfried 6/1957 |
| 806A | EMD #3128 | 5/1945 | Sold to National Metal & Steel 6/1957, to B & O #4412 |
| 806B | EMD #3136 | 5/1945 | Sold to National Metal & Steel 6/1957, to B & O #5412 |
| 807A | EMD #3129 | 5/1945 | Sold to National Metal & Steel 6/1957, to B & O #4413 |
| 807B | EMD #3137 | 5/1945 | Sold to National Metal & Steel 6/1957, to B & O #5413 |
| 808A | EMD #3130 | 5/1945 | Sold to Harold Gottfried 6/1957 |
| 808B | EMD #3138 | 5/1945 | Sold to Harold Gottfried 6/1957 |

## Class C — Freight locomotive F3 — 40 — B-B+B-B — 458,000 — 115,000 — 3,000

| | | | |
|---|---|---|---|
| 821A | EMD #3142 | 3/1948 | Sold to Erie RR 6/1957, to Erie #714A |
| 821B | EMD #3144 | 3/1948 | Sold to Erie RR 6/1957, to Erie #714B |
| 822A | EMD #3143 | 3/1948 | Sold to Erie RR 6/1957, to Erie #714D |
| 822B | EMD #3145 | 3/1948 | Sold to Erie RR 6/1957, to Erie #714C |

The company's sale list shows that Nos. 111-121 were leased to the New York Central on April 11, 1957. Nos. 111-113 were acquired from Kaplan by the Salzberg interests and stored briefly in the Unadilla Valley Ry. roundhouse at New Berlin, New York before their resale.

*page 201*

## ROSTER OF MOTOR CARS OF THE NEW YORK, ONTARIO & WESTERN RAILWAY

| No. | BUILDER | DATE | MOTOR | LENGTH | SEATS | DISPOSITION |
|---|---|---|---|---|---|---|
| 801 | Sykes | 4/15/1925 | Sterling 150 hp. (gasoline) | 43 | 38 | Retired 1/31/1939 |
| 802 | J. G. Brill | 1/23/1926 | Brill-Westinghouse 250 hp. (gasoline-electric) | 60 | 52 | Sold NH 4/1/1932 |
| 803 | J. G. Brill | 6/20/1926 | Brill-Westinghouse 250 hp. | 73 | 88 | Sold NH 12/12/1930 |
| 804 | J. G. Brill | 6/20/1926 | Brill-Westinghouse 250 hp. | 73 | 69 | Sold NH 7/24/1935 |

## LIST OF OFFICIAL AND PARLOR CARS

### Official Cars

| No. | BUILDER | DATE | LGTH | CAP | DISPOSITION |
|---|---|---|---|---|---|
| 2nd 25 | Pullman | unknown | 63 | 66 | Purchased 1903. Sold Detroit & Mackinac 1917 |
| 2nd 28 | NYO&W | 1903 | 58 | .. | Pay car |
| 2nd 30 | Jackson & Sharp | 1886 | 80 | 22 | Renumbered #135 by USRA. Steel underframe 1920's. On final roster |

### Parlor Cars

| No. | NAME | BUILDER | DATE | LGTH | CAP | DISPOSITION |
|---|---|---|---|---|---|---|
| 2nd 82 | Ulster | AC&F | 1913 | 81 | 38 | From StL-SW 1921. Rebuilt to coach 1940's. To R150. On final roster |
| 83 | Orange | AC&F | 1913 | 81 | 38 | Same as 2nd 82. To R151, 1954. On final roster. |
| 84 | Esopus | Pullman | 1908 | 72 | 37 | Retired 1946. |
| 85 | Rondout | Ohio Falls | 1897 | 72 | 35 | Rebuilt to coach 1942. Sold 1945. |
| 86 | Oriskany | Ohio Falls | 1897 | 72 | 35 | Rebuilt to coach 1942. Sold 1945. |
| 87 | Oneida | Ohio Falls | 1900 | 72 | 37 | Rebuilt to coach 1942. Sold 1945. |
| 88 | Hudson | H&H | 1904 | 73 | 42 | Retired 1946. |

| No. | Name | Builder | Year | | | Notes |
|---|---|---|---|---|---|---|
| 89 | Oswego | H&H | 1904 | 73 | 42 | Retired 1946 |
| 1st 90 | Liberty | Ohio Falls | 1898 | 60 | : | Rebuilt to coach #78, renumbered 2nd 202. Sold 1941 |
| 2nd 90 | Mamakating | H&H | 1900 | 60 | 30 | Rebuilt by H&H from 1st 93. Retired 1939. |
| 1st 91 | Walton | Ohio Falls | 1898 | 60 | : | Rebuilt to coach #79, renumbered 2nd 203. Sold 1941. |
| 2nd 91 | Wallkill | Ohio Falls | 1900 | 72 | 38 | Retired 1946. |
| 1st 92 | Delhi | Ohio Falls | 1898 | 60 | : | Rebuilt to coach #80, renumbered 2nd 204. Sold 1941. |
| 2nd 92 | Neversink | Ohio Falls | 1900 | 72 | 38 | Destroyed by fire at Winterton, 1941 |
| 1st 93 | Ellenville | Ohio Falls | 1898 | 60 | : | To 2nd 90, Mamakating |
| 2nd 93 | Willowemoc | Ohio Falls | 1900 | 72 | 35 | |
| 1st 94 | Rockland | Ohio Falls | 1898 | 60 | : | Rebuilt to coach #81, renumbered 2nd 205. Sold 1951 |
| 2nd 94 | Beaverkill | Ohio Falls | 1900 | 72 | 38 | Retired 1946. |
| 95 | Delaware | Ohio Falls | 1900 | 72 | 38 | Retired 1946. |
| 96 | Unadilla | H&H | 1901 | 72 | 42 | Retired 1946. |
| 97 | Mongaup | H&H | 1901 | 72 | 42 | Retired 1945 |
| 98 | Moodna | H&H | 1903 | 72 | 42 | Rebuilt to coach 1942. Sold 1945 |
| 99 | Chenango | H&H | 1903 | 72 | 42 | Rebuilt to coach 1942. Sold 1945 |

H&H stands for Harlan & Hollingsworth

*All the parlor cars except 2nd 82 (1st 82 was a coach) and 83 were of wood construction, with wide vestibules. The Ulster and the Orange had steel bodies and underframes, a wide vestibule and an observation platform.*

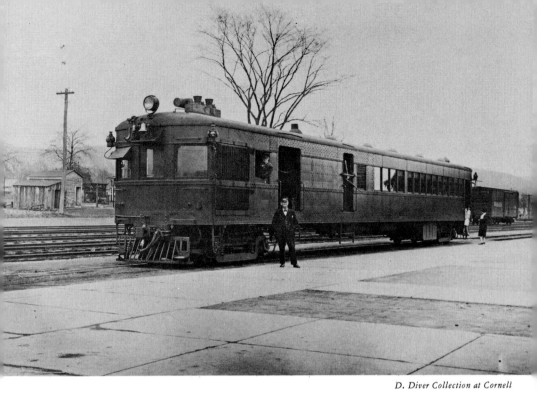

Specially constructed to accommodate mail, baggage and passengers, *#804* was a temporary answer to highway competition between Delhi and Utica.

Years before the railroad's collapse, its passenger equipment migrated south. Here is converted parlor car *Oneida* in Mexico in the 1940's.

Handsomer and more powerful than her predecessor, motor car #802 boasted a forward smoking compartment.

The O&W diesel invasion began with five of these G-E 44-tonners.

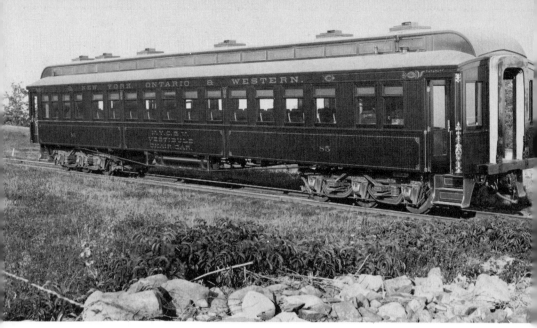

This Ohio Falls gem was the latest in travel comfort and car styling in 1897. Individual reclining chairs and elaborate gold leaf ornamentation marked it as "First-Class."

Gleaming mirrors, polished woodwork and deep plush cushions graced the interior of each reclining chair car.

| Single Fare from New York | Distance from Weehaw'n | NORTHBOUND STATIONS | 9 | 11 | 19 | 1 | 17 | 21 | 25 Sat. only | 3 | 23 | 27 Sat. only | 15 | 7 | 5 | 41 | 55 | 59 |
|---|---|---|---|---|---|---|---|---|---|---|---|---|---|---|---|---|---|---|
| | | | AM | AM | AM | AM | AM | AM | AM | no'n | PM | PM | PM | PM | PM | AM | AM | PM |
| | | New York, Desbrosses St.Lv. | 3.30 | 3.30 | 6.35 | 8.05 | 9.05 | 10.50 | 11.40 | 12.00 | 12.45 | 1.00 | 3.00 | 3.25 | 5.40 | | | |
| | | New York, West 42d Street.. | 3.45 | 3.45 | 6.45 | 8.15 | 9.15 | 11.15 | 12.00 | 12.15 | 1.00 | 1.15 | 3.15 | 3.45 | 6.00 | | | |
| | | Weehawken ¶................... | 4.00 | 4.10 | 7.00 | 8.30 | 9.30 | 11.30 | 12.15 | 12.30 | 1.20 | 1.25 | 3.30 | 4.05 | 6.10 | | | |
| \$0.80 | 32.1 | Haverstraw...... | | | | | | | | | | | | | | | | |
| 0.98 | 47.4 | West Point...... | | | 8.21 | 9.41 | | | | | | | | | | | | |
| 1.08 | 52.3 | Cornwall...... | 5.45 | 6.10 | 8.35 | 9.52 | 10.57 | 12.53 | 1.35 | 1.42 1.52 | 2.48 | 2.53 | 5.00 | 5.27 | 7.37 | | | |
| 1.14 | 55.5 | Firthcliffe...... | | 6.22 | f8.44 | | | | | | | | 5.08 | | | | | |
| 1.16 | 56.2 | Orr's Mills...... | | 6.25 | f8.46 | | | | | | | | f5.12 | | | | | |
| 1.18 | 57.8 | Meadow Brook...... | | f6.31 | f8.52 | | | | | | | | f5.17 | | | | | |
| 1.24 | 61.0 | Little Britain...... | | 6.40 | f8.58 | | | | | | | | f5.23 | | | | | |
| 1.32 | 64.6 | Rock Tavern...... | | 6.52 | f9.05 | | | | | | | | f5.30 | | | | | |
| 1.34 | 65.9 | Burnside...... | | 6.56 | f9.09 | | | | | | n3.25 | f5.34 | | | | | |
| 1.40 | 68.3 | Campbell Hall...... | 6.33 | 7.07 | 9.15 | 10.26 | | 1.27 | | | | | 5.40 | 6.02 | 8.13 | | | |
| 1.44 | 70.7 | Stony Ford...... | | 7.20 | f9.20 | | | | | | | | f5.44 | | | | | |
| 1.48 | 72.8 | Crystal Run...... | | 7.33 | f9.25 | | | | | | | | f5.48 | | | | | |
| 1.52 | 74.8 | Mechanicstown...... | | 7.39 | | | | | | | | | | | | | | |
| 1.60 | 77.8 | Middletown, Main Street.. | | | 9.36 | 10.43 | | | | | | | 5.58 | | | | | |
| 1.60 | 78.2 | MIDDLETOWN ¶....... {Ar. | 6.57 | 7.50 | 9.38 | 10.45 | 11.50 | 1.45 | 2.25 | 2.40 | 3.38 | 3.46 | 6.00 | 6.18 | 8.30 | | | |
| | | {Lv. | 7.17 | 8.25 | 9.53 | 10.55 | 12.00 | 1.55 | 2.35 | 2.50 | 3.46 | 3.56 | 6.10 | 6.30 | 8.40 | | | |
| 1.68 | 82.2 | Fair Oaks..... | | 8.35 | | | | | | | | | 6.19 | | | | | |
| 1.74 | 85.7 | Winterton..... | | 8.46 | 10f07 | | 12m12 | | | | | | 6.27 | | | | | |
| 1.80 | 88.2 | Bloomingburgh..... | | 9.01 | 10.16 | 11.15 | 12.18 | | 2.51 | 3.08 | | 4.16 | 6.35 | | | | | |
| 1.82 | 89.8 | Mamakating..... | | 9.06 | 10.22 | 11.19 | 12f22 | | | 3.12 | | n4.20 | 6.40 | | | | | |
| 1.90 | 93.1 | Summitville..... | | 9.20 | 10.40 | 11.30 | 12.33 | | | 3.23 | 4.13 | 4.30 | 6.48 | 6.56 | n9.04 | | | |
| 2.06 | 101.8 | Mountaindale..... | 8.08 | 9.47 | 11.05 | 11.49 | 12.52 | 2.40 | | 3.42 | | 4.49 | | 7.17 | | | | |
| 2.12 | 104.4 | Centreville..... | | 10.00 | 11.20 | 11.54 | 12.58 | 2.50 | | 3.49 | | 4.55 | | 7.25 | | | | |
| 2.20 | 108.0 | Fallsburgh..... | 8.55 | 10.32 | 12.05 | 1.07 | | 3.00 | 3.29 | 3.59 | | 5.06 | | 7.35 | 9.32 | | | |
| 2.26 | 111.3 | Luzon..... | | 10.43 | 11.43 | 12.12 | 1.14 | 3.08 | | 4.08 | | 5.13 | | 7.43 | | | | |
| 2.36 | 116.5 | Ferndale..... | | 11.05 | 11.54 | 12f22 | 1.24 | 3.19 | | 4.20 | | 5.26 | | 7.53 | | | | |
| 2.40 | 118.5 | Liberty..... | 9.30 | 11.20 | 12.12 | 12.29 | 1.30 | 3.25 | 3.50 | 4.35 | | 5.35 | | 8.03 | 9.54 | | | |
| 2.50 | 123.8 | Parksville..... | | 11.35 | 12.26 | 12.40 | | | | 4.46 | | 5.47 | | 8.15 | 10.16 | | | |
| 2.62 | 129.2 | Livingston Manor..... | 9.57 | 11.50 | 12.36 | 12.53 | | | | 4.55 | | 6.00 | | 8.28 | 10.18 | | | |
| 2.74 | 135.4 | Roscoe..... | 10.12 | 12.10 | | 1.08 | | | | 5.13 | | | | 8.40 | 10.26 | | | |
| 2.84 | 140.8 | Cook's Falls..... | 10.25 | 12.28 | | 1.20 | | | | 5.25 | | | | | a | | | |
| 3.00 | 148.2 | Trout Brook..... | | 12.45 | | n1.32 | | | | f5.40 | | | | | | | | |
| 3.04 | 150.4 | East Branch..... | 10.47 | 12.50 | | 1.37 | | | | 5.46 | | | | | | | | |
| 3.12 | 154.3 | Fish's Eddy..... | 10.59 | 1.00 | | 1.46 | | | | 5.55 | | | | | | | | |
| 3.22 | 159.9 | Cadosia..... | 11.17 | 1.20 | | 2.00 | | | | 6.29 | | | | | 11.05 | | | |
| 3.38 | 167.2 | Apex..... | 11f40 | 1.40 | | b | | | | f6.25 | | | | | | | | |
| 3.46 | 171.5 | Rock Rift..... | 11f48 | 1.50 | | b | | | | f6.33 | | | | | | | | |
| 3.52 | 174.3 | Beerston..... | | 1.56 | | | | | | f6.40 | | | | | | | | |
| 3.62 | 179.4 | WALTON ¶....... {Ar. | 12.05 | 2.10 | | 2.37 | | | | 6.50 | | | | 11.37 | | | | |
| | | {Lv. | 12.27 | 2.30 | | 2.42 | | | | | | | | 11.42 | | 8.05 | | |
| 3.76 | 186.6 | Northfield..... | | 3.00 | | f2.57 | | | | | | | | 12n06 | | f8.20 | | |
| 3.82 | 189.7 | Franklin..... | 1.00 | 3.17 | | 3.03 | | | | | | | | | 8.28 | | |
| 3.90 | 193.0 | Maywood..... | 1.08 | 3.28 | | 3.11 | | | | | | | | 12n12 | | 8.35 | | |
| 3.96 | 196.1 | Youngs..... | | 3.49 | | n3.16 | | | | | | | | | | f8.41 | | |
| 3.98 | 197.5 | South Unadilla..... | | 3.53 | | 3.21 | | | | | | | | | | f8.44 | | |
| 4.04 | 200.5 | SIDNEY ¶....... {Ar. | 1.25 | 4.00 | | 3.26 | | | | | | | | 12.25 | | 8.50 | | |
| | | {Lv. | | | | 3.35 | | | | | | | | 12.30 | | 9.03 | | |
| 4.10 | 203.2 | New Berlin Junction..... | | | | 3.42 | | | | | | | | | | f9.17 | | |
| 4.20 | 208.4 | Parker..... | | | | f3.53 | | | | | | | | | | 9.22 | | |
| 4.22 | 209.8 | Guilford..... | | | | 3.58 | | | | | | | | | | 9.36 | | |
| 4.36 | 216.7 | Oxford..... | | | | 4.12 | | | | | | | | | c | | | |
| 4.54 | 225.1 | NORWICH ¶........ {Ar. | | | | 4.26 | | | | | | | | 1.13 | | 9.50 | | |
| | | {Lv. | | | | 4.30 | | | | | | | | 1.23 | 7.30 | 9.54 | | 2.10 |
| 4.64 | 230.7 | Galena..... | | | | | | | | | | | | | 7.41 | 10f04 | 2.25 |
| 4.70 | 233.2 | Sherburne Four Corners..... | | | | | | | | | | | | | f7.46 | | 2.35 |
| 4.76 | 236.4 | Smyrna...... | | | | 4.49 | | | | | | | | n141 | 7.52 | 10.16 | 2.50 |
| 4.84 | 240.4 | Earlville..... | | | | 4.58 | | | | | | | | | 8.00 | 10.25 | 3.02 |
| 4.92 | 244.2 | Randallsville..... | | | | 5.13 | | | | | | | | 1.54 | 8.10 | 10.32 | 3.15 |
| 4.96 | 246.5 | Hamilton..... | | | | 5.19 | | | | | | | | 1.59 | | 10.38 | 3.23 |
| 5.00 | 248.8 | Eaton..... | | | | 5.22 | | | | | | | | | 8.23 | | |
| 5.06 | 251.5 | Morrisville..... | | | | 5.28 | | | | | | | | | 8.29 | | |
| 5.10 | 253.8 | Pratts..... | | | | 5.33 | | | | | | | | | 8.34 | | |
| 5.20 | 258.0 | Munns..... | | | | 5.46 | | | | | | | | | 8.43 | | |
| 5.20 | 258.8 | Stockbridge..... | | | | | | | | | | | | | 8.44 | | |
| 5.24 | 260.5 | Valley Mills..... | | | | f5.51 | | | | | | | | | 8.48 | | |
| 5.30 | 263.8 | Kenwood..... | | | | 5.57 | | | | | | | | | 9.00 | | |
| 5.36 | 266.1 | Castle..... | | | | 6.02 | | | | | | | | | 9.10 | | |
| 5.38 | 267.3 | ONEIDA ¶........... {Ar. | | | | 6.05 | | | | | | | | 2.37 | 9.15 | | |
| | | {Lv. | | | | 6.10 | | | | | | | | 2.46 | 9.20 | | |
| 5.42 | 269.5 | Durhamville..... | | | | | | | | | | | | | 9.25 | | |
| 5.46 | 271.6 | State Bridge..... | | | | | | | | | | | | | 9.30 | | |
| 5.54 | 275.0 | Fish Creek..... | | | | | | | | | | | | | 9.36 | | |
| 5.56 | 276.3 | Sylvan Beach(See page 13) .. | | | | 6.29 | | | | | | | | | 9.40 | | |
| 5.58 | 277.8 | North Bay..... | | | | 6.33 | | | | | | | | | 9.45 | | |
| 5.64 | 280.9 | Jewell..... | | | | f6.38 | | | | | | | | | 9.50 | | |
| 5.72 | 284.7 | Cleveland..... | | | | 6.45 | | | | | | | | | 9.57 | | |
| 5.78 | 287.4 | Bernhard's..... | | | | 6.51 | | | | | | | | | 10.03 | | |
| 5.84 | 290.9 | Constantia..... | | | | 6.57 | | | | | | | | | 10.10 | | |
| 5.92 | 294.7 | West Monroe..... | | | | 7.03 | | | | | | | | | 10.17 | | |
| 6.00 | 298.5 | Central Square..... | | | | 7.11 | | | | | | | | | 10.25 | | |
| 6.06 | 301.8 | Caughdenoy..... | | | | f7.17 | | | | | | | | | 10.32 | | |
| 6.12 | 304.8 | Pennellville..... | | | | 7.22 | | | | | | | | | 10.40 | | |
| 6.22 | 309.1 | Ingell's..... | | | | f7.30 | | | | | | | | | 10f48 | | |
| 6.28 | 312.6 | Fulton (Broadway)..... | | | | 7.36 | | | | | | | | 3.45 | 10.57 | | |
| 6.30 | 313.1 | Fulton..... | | | | 7.39 | | | | | | | | n3.47 | 11.00 | | |
| 6.38 | 317.4 | Bundy's..... | | | | f7.46 | | | | | | | | | 11f06 | | |
| 6.40 | 319.0 | Minetto..... | | | | f7.49 | | | | | | | | | 11.10 | | |
| 6.50 | 324.8 | Oswego ¶...........Ar. | | | | 8.00 | | | | | | | | 4.05 | 11.20 | | |
| | | | PM | PM | AM | PM | PM | PM | PM | PM | PM | PM | PM | PM | AM | AM | AM | PM |

Notes in columns: "No. 21, first trip June 28th" (column 21); "Last trip Aug. 31st" (column 3); "Last trip August 31st" (column 27).

For notes and reference marks see pages 16, 17 and 18.

# MAIN LINE 1907 Week Day Trains—SOUTHBOUND

| Distance from Oswego | SOUTHBOUND STATIONS | 16 | 8 | 24 | 4 | 18 | 2 | 22 | 20 | 6 | 12 | 10 | 42 | 56 | 40 | 60 |
|---|---|---|---|---|---|---|---|---|---|---|---|---|---|---|---|---|
| | | AM | AM | AM | AM | PM | AM | PM | PM | AM | AM | PM | PM | PM | AM | PM |
| ..... | Oswego ¶ .....Lv. | | | | | | 6.45 | | | 11.55 | | | 2.55 | | | |
| 5.8 | Minetto | | | | | | f6 55 | | | | | | 3.06 | | | |
| 7.4 | Bundy's | | | | | | f6.58 | | | | | | f3.09 | | | |
| 11.7 | Fulton | | | | | | 7.06 | | | 12.15 | | | 3.17 | | | |
| 12.2 | Fulton Broadway | | | | | | 7.09 | | | 12.17 | | | 3.20 | | | |
| 15.7 | Ingells | | | | | | f7.15 | | | | | | f3.25 | | | |
| 20.0 | Pennellville | | | | | | 7.25 | | | | | | 3.32 | | | |
| 23.0 | Caughdenoy | | | | | | f7.30 | | | | | | 3.37 | | | |
| 26.3 | Central Square | | | | | | 7.36 | | | | | | 3.44 | | | |
| 30.8 | West Monroe | | | | | | f7.42 | | | | | | 3.52 | | | |
| 33.9 | Constantia | | | | | | 7.51 | | | | | | 4.02 | | | |
| 37.4 | Bernhard's | | | | | | 7.58 | | | | | | 4.10 | | | |
| 40.1 | Cleveland | | | | | | 8.05 | | | 12.55 | | | 4.19 | | | |
| 43.9 | Jewell | | | | | | f8.13 | | | | | | 4.28 | | | |
| 47.0 | North Bay | | | | | | 8.19 | | | | | | 4.35 | | | |
| 48.0 | Sylvan Beach (See p. 13) | | | | | | 8.23 | | | 1.06 | | | 4.45 | | | |
| 49.8 | Fish Creek | | | | | | 8.27 | | | | | | 4.51 | | | |
| 53.2 | State Bridge | | | | | | f8.33 | | | | | | 4.58 | | | |
| 55.3 | Durhamville | | | | | | f8.38 | | | | | | 5.04 | | | |
| 57.5 | ONEIDA ¶ { Ar. | | | | | | 8.43 | | | 1.20 | | | 5.10 | | | |
| | ONEIDA ¶ { Lv. | | | | | | 8.50 | | | 1.23 | | | 5.20 | | | |
| 58.7 | Castle | | | | | | 8.53 | | | | | | 5.27 | | | |
| 61.0 | Kenwood | | | | | | 9.00 | | | | | | 5.33 | | | |
| 64.3 | Valley Mills | | | | | | f9.08 | | | | | | 5.38 | | | |
| 66.0 | Stockbridge | | | | | | | | | | | | f5.42 | | | |
| 66.8 | Munns | | | | | | 9.15 | | | | | | 5.46 | | | |
| 71.0 | Pratts | | | | | | 9.25 | | | | | | 5.55 | | | |
| 73.3 | Morrisville | | | | | | 9.32 | | | | | | 6.00 | | | |
| 76.0 | Eaton | | | | | | 9.41 | | | | | | 6.07 | | | |
| 77.8 | Hamilton | | | | | | 9.45 | | | 2.01 | | | | 6.08 | | 12.06 |
| 80.6 | RANDALLSVILLE { Ar. | | | | | | 9.55 | | | 2.05 | | | 6.15 | 6.12 | | 12.10 |
| | RANDALLSVILLE { Lv. | | | | | | 9.55 | | | 2.06 | | | 6.25 | 6.15 | | 12.15 |
| 84.4 | Earlville | | | | | | 10.05 | | | 2n11 | | | 6.35 | 6.22 | | 12.29 |
| 88.4 | Smyrna | | | | | | 10.16 | | | 2n16 | | | 6.43 | 6.29 | | 12.48 |
| 91.6 | Sherburne, Four Corners | | | | | | | | | | | | f6.49 | | | 1.02 |
| 94.1 | Galena | | | | | | | | | | | | 6.54 | | | 1.15 |
| 99.7 | NORWICH ¶ { Ar. | | | | | | 10.34 | | | 2.34 | | | 7.05 | 6.47 | | 1.25 |
| | NORWICH ¶ { Lv. | | | | | | 10.40 | | | 2.39 | | | | 6.50 | 6.55 | |
| 108.1 | Oxford | | | | | | 10.57 | | | c | | | | 7.04 | 7.30 | |
| 115.0 | Guilford | | | | | | 11.12 | | | | | | | 7.17 | 8.10 | |
| 116.4 | Parker | | | | | | 11f16 | | | | | | | | 8.20 | |
| 121.6 | New Berlin Junction | | | | | | 11.25 | | | | | | | | 8.35 | |
| 124.3 | SIDNEY { Ar. | | | | | | 11.30 | | | 3.25 | | | | 7.35 | 8.45 | |
| | SIDNEY { Lv. | | | | | | 11.35 | | | 3.29 | 10.30 | 1.25 | | 7.40 | | |
| 127.3 | South Unadilla | | | | | | 11.42 | | | | 10.40 | | | f7.47 | | |
| 128.6 | Youngs | | | | | | | | | | 10.45 | | | 7.50 | | |
| 131.8 | Maywood | | | | | | 11.54 | | | | 11.08 | | | 7.58 | | |
| 135.1 | Franklin | | | | | | 12.03 | | | 3n53 | 11.25 | | | 8.07 | | |
| 138.2 | Northfield | | | | | | 12f10 | | | | 11.45 | | | 8.16 | | |
| 145.4 | WALTON ¶ { Ar. | | | | | | 12.25 | | | 4.11 | 12.05 | 2.25 | | 8.30 | | |
| | WALTON ¶ { Lv. | | | | 8.02 | | 12.37 | | | 4.16 | 12.15 | 2.40 | | | | |
| 150.5 | Beerston | | | | f8.10 | | | | | | 12.28 | | | | | |
| 153.3 | Rock Rift | | | | f8.15 | | b | | | | 12.35 | | | | | |
| 157.6 | Apex | | | | f8.22 | | b | | | | 12.45 | | | | | |
| 164.9 | Cadosia | | | | 8.40 | | 1.20 | | | 4.50 | 1.06 | 3.27 | | | | |
| 170.5 | Fish's Eddy | | | | 8.50 | | 1.31 | | | | 1.19 | | | | | |
| 174.5 | East Branch | | | | 8.58 | | 1.40 | | | | 1.45 | 3.48 | | | | |
| 176.6 | Trout Brook | | | | f9.02 | | f1.45 | | | | 1.50 | | | | | |
| 184.0 | Cook's Falls | | | | 9.17 | | 2.01 | | | 5n18 | 2.13 | 4.09 | | | | |
| 189.4 | Roscoe | | 6.20 | | 9.29 | | 2.13 | | 4.40 | | 2.29 | 4.23 | | | | |
| 195.6 | Livingston Manor | | 6.35 | | 9.45 | | 2.28 | | 4.57 | 5.40 | 2.51 | 4.40 | | | | |
| 201.0 | Parksville | | 6.47 | | 9.57 | | 2.40 | | | | 3.05 | | | | | |
| 206.3 | Liberty | | 7.00 | | 10.14 | 2.25 | 2.55 | 4.10 | 5.19 | 5.59 | 3.25 | 5.08 | | | | |
| 208.3 | Ferndale | | 7.05 | | 10.19 | 2.30 | f3.00 | 4.15 | | | 3.31 | | | | | |
| 213.5 | Luzon | | 7.14 | | 10.31 | 2.42 | 3.12 | 4.26 | | | 3.51 | | | | | |
| 216.8 | Fallsburgh | | 7.21 | | 10.39 | 2.51 | 3.22 | 4.36 | 5.38 | 6.19 | 4.05 | 5.45 | | | | |
| 220.4 | Centreville | | 7.28 | | 10.47 | 3.00 | 3.30 | 4.45 | | | 4.25 | | | | | |
| 223.0 | Mountaindale | | 7.34 | | 10.53 | 3.07 | 3.37 | 4.52 | | | 4.31 | | | | | |
| 231.7 | Summitville | 7.05 | 7.49 | 10.55 | 11.10 | 3.28 | 3.56 | 5.08 | 6.05 | 6.46 | 4.54 | 6.17 | | | | |
| 235.0 | Mamakating | 7.12 | d | | 11.18 | | 4.04 | 5.15 | | | 5.05 | | | | | |
| 236.6 | Bloomingburgh | 7.17 | | | 11.23 | 3.40 | 4.09 | 5.20 | n6.14 | | 5.25 | | | | | |
| 239.1 | Winterton | f7.22 | | | 11f28 | | n4.14 | | | | 5.33 | | | | | |
| 242.5 | Fair Oaks | f7.28 | | | | | | | | | 5.41 | | | | | |
| 246.6 | MIDDLETOWN ¶ { Ar. | 7.35 | 8.15 | 11.23 | 11.40 | 3.55 | 4.26 | 5.40 | 6.30 | 7.13 | 5.50 | 6.50 | | | | |
| | MIDDLETOWN ¶ { Lv. | 7.45 | 8.25 | 11.33 | 11.50 | 4.05 | 4.36 | 5.50 | 6.40 | 7.23 | 6.00 | 7.05 | | | | |
| 247.1 | Middletown, Main Street | 7.47 | | | | | 4.38 | | | | | | | | | |
| 250.0 | Mechanicstown | | | | | | | | | | 6.10 | | | | | |
| 252.0 | Crystal Run | f7.56 | | | | | f4.48 | | | | 6.20 | | | | | |
| 254.1 | Stony Ford | f8.00 | | | | | f4.52 | | | | 6.29 | | | | | |
| 256.5 | Campbell Hall | 8.06 | 8.42 | | | | 4.58 | | | | 6.45 | 7.43 | | | | |
| 258.9 | Burnside | f8.11 | | | | | f5.03 | | | | 7.03 | | | | | |
| 260.2 | Rock Tavern | f8.14 | | | | | f5.06 | | | | 7.14 | | | | | |
| 263.0 | Little Britain | f8.22 | | | | | f5.14 | | | | 7.27 | | | | | |
| 267.0 | Meadow Brook | f8.28 | | | | | f5.21 | | | | 7.38 | | | | | |
| 268.6 | Orr's Mills | f8.31 | | | | | f5.24 | | | | 7.42 | | | | | |
| 269.3 | Firthcliffe | 8.33 | | | 12n29 | | 5.28 | | 7n14 | | 7.46 | | | | | |
| 272.5 | Cornwall | 8.40 | 9.08 | 12.16 | 12.35 | 4.50 | 5.34 | 6.45 | 7.20 | 8.05 | 7.55 | 8.25 | | | | |
| 277.4 | West Point | | 9.18 | 12.46 | | | 5.46 | | | | 8.17 | | | | | |
| 292.6 | Haverstraw | | 9.41 | 1.10 | | | | | | | 8.44 | | | | | |
| 324.8 | Weehawken ¶ .....Ar. | 10.05 | 10.30 | 1.35 | 2.00 | 6.15 | 7.05 | 8.10 | 8.45 | 9.30 | 10.10 | 10.20 | | | | |
| ..... | New York, W. 42d St. " | 10.15 | 10.40 | 1.45 | 2.15 | 6.25 | 7.15 | 8.30 | 9.00 | 9.45 | 10.40 | 10.40 | | | | |
| ..... | N. Y., Desbrosses St. " | 10.35 | 11.00 | 2.00 | 2.30 | 6.40 | 7.30 | 8.45 | 9.15 | 10.00 | 11.00 | 11.00 | | | | |
| | | AM | AM | PM | PM | PM | PM | PM | PM | PM | PM | PM | PM | PM | AM | PM |

Note (vertical, column 22): No. 22 First trip June 28th.

For notes and reference marks see pages 19 and 20.

# BIBLIOGRAPHY

THE MAJOR printed sources of this history are as follows:

*Annual Reports of the Board of Railroad Commissioners*, Albany, James B. Lyon, 1884-1906.

*Annual Reports of the New York, Ontario and Western Railway Company*, 1880-1956.

BEST, GERALD M., "History and Motive Power of the New York, Ontario and Western Railroad [sic]," *Railway and Locomotive Historical Society Bulletin No. 40*, May 1936.

BEST, GERALD M., *Minisink Valley Express: A History of the Port Jervis, Monticello & New York Railroad and its Predecessors*, Beverly Hills, Gerald M. Best, 1957.

CHILD, HAMILTON, compiler, *Gazeteer and Business Directory of Sullivan County, N. Y.,* Syracuse, Hamilton Child, 1872.

*Dispatcher's Diaries*, Norwich, 1890-1940.

GROSS, H. H., "Shawangunk Barrier," *Railroad Magazine*, September 1946.

HARLOW, ALVIN F., *The Road of the Century: The Story of the New York Central*, New York, Creative Age Press, 1947.

HUNGERFORD, EDWARD, "The Railway Systems of New York," *History of the State of New York*, edited by Alexander C. Flick, Vol. VI, New York, Columbia University Press, 1934.

HUNGERFORD, EDWARD, *Men and Iron: The History of New York Central*, New York, Thomas Y. Crowell Co., 1938.

HUNGERFORD, EDWARD, *The Story of the Rome, Watertown and Ogdensburgh Railroad*, New York, Robert M. McBride & Co., 1922.

JONES, ELIOT, *The Anthracite Coal Combination in the United States*, Cambridge, Harvard University Press, 1914.

KESSLER, WILLIAM CONRAD, "The Railroad Age in Madison County," *New York History,* January 1941.

KESSLER, WILLIAM CONRAD, "Report on the New York, Ontario and Western Railway," mimeographed, 1950.

LEE, HARDY CAMPBELL, *A History of the Railroads in Tompkins County,* Ithaca, DeWitt Historical Society of Tompkins County, 1947.

LUCAS, WALTER ARNDT, *The History of the New York, Susquehanna and Western Railroad,* New York, Railroadians of America, 1939.

"The Mighty O&W," *The Courier Magazine,* October 1953.

MORGAN, DAVID P., "He Sold Streamlining," *Trains,* July 1952.

NEUSSER, A. V. and PEARCE, C. E., "The NYO&W," *Trains,* August 1942.

"Obituary of an Old Woman," *Trains,* July 1957.

PIERCE, HARRY H., *Railroads of New York,* Cambridge, Harvard University Press, 1953.

POOR, HENRY V., *Manuals of Railroads,* New York, annual.

PRATT, GEORGE WILLIAM, *History of the New York, Ontario and Western Railroad* [sic], Cornell University Thesis (unpublished), 1942.

QUINLAN, JAMES ELDRIDGE, *History of Sullivan County,* Liberty, 1873.

SLAWSON, GEORGE C., *The History of the New York and Oswego Midland Railroad,* typewritten manuscript, 1942.

SMITH, JAMES H., *History of Chenango and Madison Counties 1784-1880,* Syracuse, D. Mason & Co., 1881.

SNYDER, CARL, *American Railways as Investments,* New York, The Moody Corporation, 1907.

SNYDER, CHARLES M., *Dewitt C. Littlejohn: A Study in Leadership in Oswego in the Nineteenth Century,* (Part I in *Twentieth Publication of the Oswego County Historical Society,* 1957; the remainder in manuscript).

*State Engineer's Reports on Railroads,* Albany, Weed, Parsons and Co., 1870-1882.

UNITED STATES INTERSTATE COMMERCE COMMISSION, *Finance Docket No. 11662.* (New York, Ontario & Western Railway Company Reorganization.)

UNITED STATES INTERSTATE COMMERCE COMMISSION, *Valuation Docket 192: New York, Ontario and Western Railway Company,* 1929.

# INDEX

Only subjects in the main text have been entered here. Illustrations are listed on pages iv- vi and the Appendix has equipment information arranged in an accessible tabular format.